THE
HEBREWS
AND THE
TIME OF
THE END

ALAN T. HARRIS

ISBN Softback: 979-8-9922525-2-1
ISBN eBook: 979-8-9922525-3-8
Library of Congress Control Number: 2026902631

All Scripture is taken from the Authorized King James Version of the Holy Bible. The bolding and underlining of certain words are added by the author for emphasis and do not represent an alteration of the public domain text.

Interior Layout: Megan Leid
Publisher: LionStar Publishing LLC
Website: https://lookingforthatblessedhope.com/
Printed in the United States of America

TABLE OF CONTENTS

PREFACE

As the world approaches closer to what many call Daniel's 70th week, more commonly known as the Tribulation period, the further away people, including Christians, are moving themselves from God and His Word. While we have seen a small uptick in revivals here and there, the general direction is as prophesied in 1 Timothy. Where in this long list of adjectives is it not obvious today?

> *This know also, that in the **last days perilous times shall come**. For men shall be lovers of their own selves, covetous, boasters, proud, blasphemers, disobedient to parents, unthankful, unholy, Without natural affection, trucebreakers, false accusers, incontinent, fierce, despisers of those that are good, Traitors, heady, highminded, **lovers of pleasures more than lovers of God; Having a form of godliness, but denying the power thereof:** from such turn away. 1 Timothy 3:1-5*

The Hamas attack on Israel on October 7th, 2024, marked a pivotal event in world history. From that point forward, much of the world and many "prominent Christians" have turned against Israel in every fashion imaginable. It will continue to get worse until sometime soon, the world will find itself immersed in that 70th week, an inconceivable time that is by and large about the Jewish people.

In this book I have attempted to define two major themes. The Falling Away and the widely researched book of 2 Thessalonians chapter two. All of this started when I was studying the alarming verse in Hebrews 10:26 that states: *"For if we sin wilfully after that we have received the knowledge of the truth, **there remaineth no more sacrifice for sins**,"*. After much study, one discovery continued to lead to another until the idea for this book had been set.

The most common consensus for the Falling Away is that of the Church falling into apostasy. Another common view refers to it as the departure of the Church via the Rapture. Recently, a new suggestion has emerged for the Falling Away and suggest it is the apostasy in a spiritual sense of the Jewish acceptance of the Antichrist by signing the 7-year covenant which includes the ability to have temple sacrifices. I will attempt to make the case that none of these are correct but it is rather an ominous rebellion that will affect all people of the world and does not occur until the Tribulation begins.

I will also attempt to unscramble the rather complicated chapter two of 2 Thessalonians in a way perhaps the reader is not familiar with, shedding much light on The Time of The End. Ultimately, it is up to the reader, as it should be with all dissertations on scripture from any author, to heed what Acts 17:11 says, *"These were more noble than those in Thessalonica, in that they received the word with all readiness of mind, and searched the scriptures daily, <u>whether those things were so.</u>"*.

TESTAMENT VS COVENANT

Before we get to the crux of the matter, a few patterns and terms must first be defined to understand the Time of the End. One must have discernment concerning testaments and covenants as these two concepts are often confused within the Church. Perhaps most are familiar with testaments, specifically the Old and the New. It is essential to recognize that a Testament specifically refers to how an individual soul is saved.

The word "testament" is only used in the New Testament fourteen times. The Old Testament was the book of the law given to Moses as we see in the verse below and is the only time "Old Testament" is used.

*"But their minds were blinded: for until this day remaineth the same vail untaken away in the **reading** of the **old testament;** which vail is done away in Christ" 2 Corinthians 3:14.*

The book of the law contained a total of 613 laws. Six the number for man; thirteen the number for sin, judgement and ultimately death. In other words, the law was a reminder, a warning that man is sinful and will be judged accordingly. Theoretically, a man could be "saved" if he was able to obey all 613 laws to his death without failure of any instance. However, we know that was not possible for any man except Jesus who came to fulfil the law and the prophets. *" Think not that I am come to destroy the law, or the prophets: I am **<u>not come to destroy</u>**, but to **fulfil**."* *Matthew 5:17.* Since no man could fully obey the law, the Old Testament required a **blood sacrifice**, hence the Levite priest sacrificed once per year for the sins of the nation of Israel on the Day of Atonement. It was designated as an "everlasting statue" and will be instituted again during the Millennial Reign where Ezekiel chapters 40-48 prophetically outlines a future temple in Jerusalem with an active sacrificial system. *"And this shall be an* **everlasting statute** *unto you, to make an* **atonement** *for the* <u>children of Israel</u> *for all their* **sins once a year.** *And he did as the LORD commanded Moses." Leviticus 16:34.*

> *"All the people of the land shall give this oblation for the prince in Israel. And it shall be the prince's part to give* **burnt offerings, and meat offerings, and drink offerings,** *in the feasts, and in the new moons, and in the sabbaths, in all solemnities of*

*the house of Israel: he shall prepare the **sin offering, and the meat offering, and the burnt offering, and the peace offerings,** to make **reconciliation** for the <u>house of Israel</u>." Ezekiel 45:16-17*

*"Whereupon **neither the first testament was dedicated <u>without blood</u>.**" Hebrews 9:18*

A Testament cannot exist unless there is the death of a testator. Those that died as "saved" under the Old Testament would have to wait on the death of Jesus Christ for their redemption of sin. For only by the blood of Jesus can one be saved. Consequently, the reason Paradise was located on the opposite side of the gulf in Hell during the Old Testament time (Luke 16:25-26). The New Testament abolished the law for those entering the Church by the blood of Jesus including Messianic Jews.

*"And for this cause he is the mediator of the **new testament, that by means of death,** for the **redemption of the transgressions** that were **under the <u>first testament</u>,** they which are called might receive the promise of eternal inheritance." Hebrews 9:15*

*"For where a **testament is,** there must also of necessity be the **death** of the **testator.**" Hebrews 9:16*

"For this is my blood of the new testament, which is shed for many for the remission of sins." Matthew 26:28

"In whom we have redemption through his blood, even the forgiveness of sins:" Colossians 1:14

"Having abolished in his flesh the enmity, even the law of commandments contained in ordinances; for to make in himself of twain one new man, so making peace;" Eph 2:15

Covenants are promises/agreements of many things. No covenant was given to the Church except for the Noahic Covenant, which was determined upon all people of the world. It was **unconditional** and God's promise never to destroy the earth again with a flood as He did twice previously. The other three covenants were given to the Hebrews starting with the Abrahamic Covenant, and then to the Israelites including the Mosaic Covenant and the Davidic Covenant. These latter two covenants apply to the Jewish people as a nation, the state of Israel.

The Abrahamic Covenant was the **unconditional** promise of God to Abraham including his offspring and seed. It included the promise of land as an everlasting possession (Gen 12:7). The borders of Israel today will in the future expand to the original borders God promised Abraham. To Abrahams descendants of Isaac and Jacob was promised a *"great nation"* (Gen 12:2), and his seed would become as numerous as the stars (Gen 15:5). Through Abraham all families of earth would be blessed (Gen 12:3) and those in Christ are the seed of Abraham and *"heirs according to the promise"* (Gal 3:29). The Abrahamic Covenant was the foundation for the Mosaic and Davidic Covenants and an **everlasting** covenant (Gen 17:7).

The Mosaic Covenant named after Moses, was given to the children of Israel after deliverance from slavery in Egypt. The covenant contained the Books of the Law, the Torah, or the first five books of the bible and promises of various blessings or curses depending on obedience or disobedience of the children of Israel. It is a **conditional** covenant. Within this covenant resides the **Old Testament.** The conditional Mosaic Covenant is the reason the history of the children of Israel is littered with destruction and chaos, from the time of their deliverance out of Egypt into the future Tribulation period by way of their disobedience.

The Davidic covenant was given to King David. It is another **unconditional** covenant promise of God to establish and give the ultimate seed of Abraham and a descendant of David, Jesus, an eternal dynasty and kingdom of which He will reign forever as *"Prince of Kings of the Earth"* (Rev 1:5) while David will reign as King over the nation of Israel forever observing the statues. (2 Sam 7 12-17) *"And **David** my servant shall be **king** over them; and they all shall have one shepherd: they shall also **walk in** *my judgments, and observe my statutes, and do them."* Ez 37:24. *"Once have I sworn by my holiness that I will not lie unto David. His seed shall endure for ever, and his throne as the sun before me. It shall be established for ever as the moon, and as a faithful witness in heaven. Selah."* Psalms 89:35-37

There is a clear distinction between the Church with the *bride* of Christ, and the Nation of Israel now and forever. It will become more evident as we move forward. We must rightly divide or we will confuse our doctrine which the enemy encourages. *"Study to shew thyself approved unto God, a workman that needeth not to be ashamed, rightly dividing the word of truth."* 2 Timothy 2:15

As Christians, we are commanded to support Israel (Gen 12:3). The children of Israel today are God's chosen people but **not** for all things at all times, because of their disdain for the **Mosaic Covenant**. There are times when God has and will again "hide His face" from them. God had even given Israel a bill of divorce during the reign of King Josiah which eventually would include Judah.

"The LORD said also unto me in the days of Josiah the king, Hast thou seen that which backsliding Israel hath done? she is gone up upon every high mountain and under every green tree, and there hath played the harlot. And I said after she had done all these things, Turn thou unto me.

*But she returned not. And her **treacherous sister Judah** saw it. And I saw, when for all the causes whereby **backsliding Israel committed adultery** I had **put her away**, and given her a **bill of divorce**; yet her treacherous sister **Judah feared not**, but went and **played the harlot also**." Jer 3:6-8*

The book of Hosea further emphasizes this tragedy. God speaking to the prophet Hosea instructed him to marry a *"wife of whoredoms"* because *" the land hath committed great whoredom"* (Hosea 1:2). She had a daughter named Lo–ruhamah for God said," *I will **no more have mercy** upon the house of Israel"* Hosea 1:6. The prophets wife conceived again, *"Now when she had weaned Lo–ruhamah, she conceived, and bare a son. Then said God, Call his name Lo–ammi: for **ye are not my people**, and **I will not be your God**."* Hosea 1:8-9. The divorce is confirmed, *"Plead with your mother, plead: for **she is not my wife, neither am I her husband**: let her therefore put away her whoredoms out of her sight, and her adulteries from between her breasts;"* Hosea 2:2.

Many will refer to Paul's statement in Romans 11:1 to justify that Israel today are still the people of God. The word "cast" is a very powerful word and if we look at the meaning, the context of which Paul uses it becomes obvious. When something is cast it means permanent, that is why Paul says, *"God forbid"* immediately after *"cast"*.

Lucifer was cast permanently from the mountain of God, Ez 28:16 and will be cast permanently into the lake of fire and brimstone, Revelation 20:10. *"But the children of the kingdom shall be **cast out into outer darkness:** there shall be weeping and gnashing of teeth."* Matthew 8:12. Even though He has turned His face from them, God has always retained a remnant.

> *"I say then, Hath God **cast away** his people? **God forbid.** For I also am an Israelite, of the seed of Abraham, of the tribe of Benjamin. God **hath <u>not</u> cast away his people** which he foreknew. Wot ye not what the scripture saith of Elias? how he maketh intercession to God against Israel, saying, Lord, they have killed thy prophets, and digged down thine altars; and I am left alone, and they seek my life. But what saith the answer of God unto him? I have **reserved to myself seven thousand men**, who have not bowed the knee to the image of Baal. Even so then **at this present time** also **there is a remnant** according to the election of grace."* Romans 11:1-5

> *"For thus saith the LORD; Sing with gladness for Jacob, and shout among the chief of the nations: publish ye, praise ye, and say, O LORD, **save thy people, the remnant of Israel.**"* Jer 31:7

God is faithful to His Word and will not forget the Abrahamic and Davidic Covenant. He will eventually bring them all back as a people betrothed to Him again forever with a new covenant.

Another distinction should be noted between the ***bride of <u>Christ</u>***, both Jew and gentile saved during the Church age that will obtain resurrected bodies, and the Jewish people ***betrothed*** to ***<u>God</u>*** that survive the Tribulation and enter the Millennial Reign. The bible is not clear if the Jewish remnant and other nations receive resurrected bodies at the end of the Millennium, but perhaps they are rather the "earthly" people with physical bodies that will be sustained by other means mentioned in Revelation, hence the meaning of "sow her unto me in the earth". However, it is clear the New Heaven and New Earth at the end of the Millennium will have no end to the increase of His government, the Father's Kingdom.

> *"And in that day will I **make a covenant** for them with the beasts of the field, and with the fowls of heaven, and with the creeping things of the ground: and I **will break the bow and the sword and the battle out of the earth**, and will make them to **lie down safely**. And I **will betroth thee unto me for ever**; yea, I **will betroth thee unto me in righteousness**, and in judgment, and in loving-kindness, and in mercies. I will even betroth thee*

*unto me in faithfulness: and thou shalt know the LORD. And it shall come to pass in that day, I will hear, saith the LORD, I will hear the heavens, and they shall **hear the earth**; And the earth shall hear the corn, and the wine, and the oil; and they shall hear Jezreel. And I will <u>sow her unto me</u> in the earth; and I will have mercy upon her that **had not** obtained mercy; and I will say to them **which <u>were not</u> my people, Thou art my people**; and they shall say, **Thou art my God.***" Hosea 2:18-23

*"For unto us a child is born, unto us a son is given: and the **government** shall be upon his shoulder: and his name shall be called Wonderful, Counsellor, The mighty God, The **everlasting Father**, The Prince of Peace. Of the **increase of his government and peace** there shall be **no end,** upon the **throne of David,** and **upon his kingdom,** to order it, and to establish it **with judgment** and **with justice** from henceforth **even for ever.** The zeal of the LORD of hosts will perform this.* Is 9:6-7

Perhaps even more tragic is the Jewish people would also reject the "**New Testament**" given to them as a *nation*. It is the **Gospel** with the indwelling of the Holy Ghost distinct from the Old Testament of works under the Mosaic law.

Notice the New Testament was intended for the house of Israel only during the beginning of Jesus' ministry. *"But he answered and said, I am not sent **but unto the lost <u>sheep</u>** of the <u>**house of Israel**</u>." Matt 15:24.* Later in His ministry it would be taken from them and given to the gentiles. Reading Romans 11:11-27 will provide a better context.

*"Jesus answered them, I told you, and ye believed not: the works that I do in my Father's name, they bear witness of me. But **ye believe not,** because **ye are not of my <u>sheep</u>,** as I said unto you." John 10:25-26*

*"Jesus saith unto them, Did ye never read in the scriptures, **The stone which the builders rejected,** the same is become the head of the corner: this is the Lord's doing, and it is marvellous in our eyes? Therefore say I unto you, **The kingdom of God <u>shall be taken from you</u>,** and given to a <u>**nation**</u> (gentiles) bringing forth the fruits thereof." Matthew 21:42-43*

*"I say then, Have they stumbled that they should fall? **God forbid:** but rather through their fall **salvation is come unto the Gentiles,** for to provoke them to jealousy." Rom 11:11*

*"He came unto **his own,** and his own **received him not.**" John 1:11*

This rejection of the New Testament was prophesied in Zechariah 11. They Jews at the time of Christ's ministry on earth were constantly in disbelief (Matt 13:58); an incurable, carnal minded people which Jesus rejected leaving their house desolate (Matt 23:38).

> *"Then said I, I will not feed you: that that dieth,* **let it die***; and that that is to be cut off,* **let it be cut off***; and let the rest eat every one the flesh of another." Zec 11:9*

Jesus would no longer be a shepherd to them and prophesied they would accept the Antichrist, *"I am come in my Father's name, and* **ye receive me not***: if another shall come in his own name,* **him ye will receive***." John 5:43.*

Continuing in Zechariah below, "Beauty" refers to the Jewish temple at the time of the Crucifixion. It was cut asunder by the Romans in 70 A.D. The phrase, "broken in that day" was fulfilled the exact day Jesus told them, *"The kingdom of God shall be taken from you",* Matt 21:43 and when God broke His covenant. "Bands" is the ruin of their civil state, by breaking the brotherhood between Judah and Israel, and reviving animosities and contention among them, as in times past between Judah and Israel. A people without God, left to ruin, to eventually fall under the hand of a "foolish shepherd", an "idol shepherd", the Antichrist.

*"And I took **my staff**, even **Beauty**, and **cut it asunder**, that I might <u>break my covenant</u> which I had made with all the people. And it was **broken in that day**: and so the poor of the flock that waited upon me knew that it was the word of the LORD. And I said unto them, If ye think good, give me my price; and if not, forbear. So they weighed for my **price thirty pieces of silver**. And the LORD said unto me, Cast it unto the potter: a goodly price that I was prised at of them. And I took the thirty pieces of silver, and cast them to the potter in the house of the LORD. Then I **cut asunder** mine **other staff**, even **Bands**, that I might **break the brotherhood between Judah and Israel.***" Zec 11:10-14

*"And the LORD said unto me, Take unto thee yet the instruments of a **foolish shepherd**. For, lo, I will raise up a shepherd in the land, which shall not visit those that be cut off, neither shall seek the young one, nor heal that that is broken, nor feed that that standeth still: but **he shall eat the flesh of the fat, and tear their claws in pieces.***"* Zec 11:15-16

*Woe to the **idol shepherd** that **leaveth the flock**! the sword shall be upon his arm, and upon his* *right eye: his arm shall be clean dried up, and his right eye shall be utterly darkened. Zechariah 11:17*

*There is coming a day for the world and specifically for the Jewish people when "there **remaineth no more sacrifice for sins**" Heb 10:26.*

THE KINGDOM OF HEAVEN & THE KINGDOM OF GOD

Two distinct periods are awaited to take place between the occurrence of the rapture and the conclusion of the Tribulation. The Day of Christ will fall into the Kingdom of God, and the Day of the Lord will bring in the Kingdom of Heaven on earth during the Millennial Reign. Our initial focus will be on the Kingdom of Heaven and the Kingdom of God.

There is considerable confusion regarding the distinction between the Kingdom of Heaven and the Kingdom of God. These two kingdoms exhibit notable differences from one another. This doctrine is not new; dispensational theologians from the 19th and 20th centuries recognized the distinction, and many books cover this topic in detail. The two kingdoms have been mingled together leading to unsound teachings within the church today, especially concerning the book of Matthew. For wherever the Word becomes a little challenging, man will insert his own interpretation to the benefit of the enemy, sowing more confusion. This confusion is like the teaching of Replacement Theology, the view that the Church has superseded or replaced the Jewish people as God's chosen people. While not the topic of this book, it is vital to understand the two kingdoms for context.

> *"Whom shall he **teach knowledge?** and whom shall he make to **understand doctrine?** **them that are weaned from the milk,** and drawn from the breasts. For precept must be upon precept, **precept upon precept; line upon line,** line upon line; here a little, and there a little:" Is 28:9-10*

Perhaps the most definitive difference of the kingdoms is noted in 1 Corinthians 15:50, *"Now this I say, brethren, that **flesh and blood cannot inherit** the **kingdom of God;** neither doth corruption inherit incorruption."*. Unless one receives a resurrected body, one that is uncorruptible, they cannot enter the Kingdom of God. It requires one to believe and repentant towards God to enter His kingdom. It is the spiritual rule of God over all beings whether in heaven or hell. For the believer on earth, the Kingdom of God resides within you. The Kingdom of God refers to divine authority, power, and glory encompassing all creation, rather than being confined to a specific place.

*"For the **kingdom of God** is not meat and drink; but righteousness, and peace, and joy **in the Holy Ghost.**" Romans 14:17*

*"But the hour cometh, and now is, when the true worshippers shall **worship** the **Father** in **spirit** and in **truth**: for the Father seeketh such to worship him. **God is a Spirit**: and they that worship him **must worship him in spirit** and in truth." John 4:23-24*

*"And when he was demanded of the Pharisees, **when** the kingdom of God **should come**, he answered them and said, The kingdom of God **cometh not with observation**: Neither shall they say, Lo here! or, lo there! for, behold, the **kingdom of God is within you**." Luke 17:20-21*

*"Jesus answered and said unto him, Verily, verily, I say unto thee, Except a man be **born again**, he **cannot see** the **kingdom of God**. Nicodemus saith unto him, How can a man be born when he is old? can he enter the second time into his mother's womb, and be born? Jesus answered, Verily, verily, I say unto thee, Except a man be **born of water and of the Spirit**, he cannot **enter** into the kingdom of God. That which is born of the flesh is flesh; and that which is born of the Spirit is*

spirit. Marvel not that I said unto thee, Ye must be born again." John 3:3-7

The Kingdom of Heaven

Likewise, the Kingdom of Heaven is physical, earthly, and institutional. It is the coming 1,000-year Millennial Reign of Heaven's rule that will come down to **reign** on the earth. It is the setting up of the Davidic Covenant where King David will rule the nation of Israel forever. Those that survive the Tribulation will enter the Kingdom of Heaven with a physical body, soul, and spirit, giving birth, while physical death still remains in existence. Jesus will reside as *"Prince of Kings of the Earth"* (Rev 1:5).

> *"And the **LORD shall be king** over all the earth: in that day shall there be one LORD, and his name one." Zec 14:9*

A distinction must be also made between the Church vs the Old Testament vs the Tribulation Saints, those that die and have not worshipped or taken the mark of the beast. All will receive **resurrected bodies** to reign on earth, but only those that live and die during the Church age, that is from Pentecost to the Rapture, will be as the **bride of Christ.** The Old Testament and Tribulation Saints will be **friends** of the **Bridegroom,** *"He that hath the bride is the bridegroom: but the friend of the bridegroom, which standeth and heareth him, rejoiceth greatly..." John 3:29.* They will be **guests** at the wedding and at the marriage supper in the Kingdom of Heaven, *"and he saith unto me, Write, **Blessed are they** which are <u>called</u> unto the **marriage supper** of the Lamb.."* Rev 19:9. Those that survive the Tribulation to the very end with physical bodies, are allowed as guests to the wedding and marriage supper or "cast out" under certain conditions outlined in the Kingdom parables in Matthew. If the children of the Kingdom of God (resurrected bodies) are the **same** as those in the Kingdom of Heaven, why then are they "**cast** out into outer darkness"?

> *And I say unto you, That many shall **come from the east** and **west**, and shall sit down with **Abraham**, and Isaac, and **Jacob**, in the kingdom of heaven. But the **children of the kingdom** shall be **cast out into outer darkness**: there shall be weeping and gnashing of teeth. Matt 8:11-12*

God in His omnipotence, would not confuse us in His choice of wording. The phrase "kingdom of heaven('s)" is **only** used in the book of Matthew, a total of 33 times, perhaps once for each year of the Lord's life. Matthew is a "Kingdom" book and presents Jesus as a King. John the Baptist first preached the **Gospel of the Kingdom,** *"In those days came John the Baptist, preaching in the wilderness of Judaea, And saying, **Repent ye:** for the **kingdom of heaven is at hand.**"* Matt 3:1-2. Repentance in this context was not meant for the individual but for the **nation** of Israel to prepare for the setting up of the Kingdom. Jesus preached both kingdoms after John the Baptist was cast into prison and eventually beheaded. *"Now when Jesus had heard that **John was cast into prison**, he departed into **Galilee;"** "From that time Jesus began to preach, and to say, **Repent: for the kingdom of heaven is at hand.**"* Matt 4:12, 17. *"Now after that **John was put in prison**, Jesus came into **Galilee**, preaching the **gospel of the kingdom of God**, And saying, The time is fulfilled, and the **kingdom of God is at hand: repent ye, and believe the gospel.**"* Mark 1:14-15

The Kingdom of Heaven is for the Jewish people and Jesus commanded His disciples as such.

*"These twelve Jesus sent forth, and commanded them, saying, **Go not into the way of the Gentiles**, and into any city of the Samaritans **enter ye not**: But go rather to the **lost sheep of the house of Israel**. And as ye go, preach, saying, **The kingdom of heaven is at hand.**"* Matt 10:5-7. The Kingdom of Heaven was offered to the **nation of Israel** only and meant to come shortly after the crucifixion, but it was rejected by the Jews. As the kingdom was taken away by violence, King Jesus will return the favor at the end of the Tribulation. And from the days of ***John the Baptist*** until now the ***kingdom of heaven*** suffereth ***violence***, and ***the violent take it by force.***" Mat 11:12. There is never "violence" within the spiritual rule of the Kingdom of God.

Just before the Ascension, the disciples asked Jesus, *"When they therefore were come together, they asked of* *him, saying, Lord, wilt thou at this time **restore again the kingdom to Israel?*** Acts 1:6. *Jesus answered, "And he said unto them, It is not for you to **know the times or the seasons**, which the Father hath put in his own power. But **ye shall receive power**, after that the **Holy Ghost is come upon you:** and ye shall be witnesses unto me both in Je-rusalem, and in all Judæa, and in Samaria, and unto the uttermost part of the earth."* Acts 1:7-8. The age of the Church was about to begin, postponing the Kingdom of Heaven until a much later time.

If you understand the difference between the two kingdoms, the many parables in Matthew will begin to make more sense. The twelve parables focus on "works" and "faith," describing which Jewish people are accepted or denied entry to the Kingdom of Heaven.

Matthew 22 describes the Bridegroom's marriage to the Church on earth within the Kingdom of Heaven, following the Tribulation. It is unlikely that a King focused on avenging rebellious subjects would choose to marry His beloved bride during this period.

*And Jesus answered and spake unto them again by parables, and said, **The <u>kingdom of heaven</u>** is like unto a certain **king** (God), which **made a marriage for his son** (Jesus), And **sent forth his servants** to **call them** that were bidden to the wedding: and they would not come (Jews at the* time of Christ reject John the Baptist, Apostles message). *Again, he sent forth other servants, saying, Tell them which are bidden, Behold, I have prepared my dinner: my oxen and my fatlings are killed, and all things are ready: come unto the marriage. But **they made light of it**, and went their ways, one to his farm, another to his merchandise: And the remnant took his servants, and entreated them spitefully, and **slew them**.* (Jews killed Christians during that time) *But when the **king heard** thereof, he **was wroth**: and he **sent forth his armies**, and **destroyed those murderers**, and **burned up their city*** (70 A.D., Jerusalem destroyed and burnt by Romans). ***Then saith he to his servants*** (144,000), *The **wedding is ready*** (Rev19), *but **they which were bidden*** (Jews at time of Christ) ***were not worthy. Go ye therefore into the highways*** (all nations), ***and as many as ye shall find, bid to the marriage.*** *So those servants went out into the highways, and gathered together all as many as they found, **both bad and good: and the wedding was furnished** with **guests*** (survivors, end of Tribulation). *Matt 22:1-10*

*And when the **king came*** (His 2nd coming) *in to see the **guests**, he saw there a man which **had not*** *on a **wedding garment**: And he saith unto him, Friend, how camest thou in hither **not having a wedding garment**? And he was speechless. Then said the **king** to **the servants** (angels in this case, Matt 25 below), Bind him hand and foot, and take him away, and **cast him into outer darkness**; there shall be weeping and gnashing of teeth. For many are called, but few are chosen. Matt 22:11-14*

This casting into outer darkness of those found without the wedding garment, a garment of righteousness, happens at the time of the sheep and goat judgement.

*"When the **Son of man shall come in his glory**, and all the holy angels with him, then shall he sit upon the throne of his glory: And before him **shall be gathered all nations: and he shall separate them** one from another, as a shepherd **divideth** his **sheep** from the **goats**: And he shall set the sheep on his right hand, but the goats on the left. Then shall the King say unto them on his right hand, **Come, ye blessed** of my Father, **inherit the kingdom** prepared for you from the foundation of the world:" Matt 25:31-34*

"And the King shall answer and say unto them, Verily I say unto you, Inasmuch as ye have done

*it unto one of the least of these my brethren, ye have done it unto me. Then shall he say also unto them on the left hand, **Depart** from me, **ye cursed**, into **everlasting fire**, prepared for the devil and his angels:"* Matt 25:40-41

Jesus gives a clear warning in Revelation concerning His return and the wedding garment.

*"Behold, **I come as a thief**. Blessed is he that watcheth, and **keepeth his garments**, lest he **walk naked**, and they see his **shame**."* Revelation 16:15

Perhaps the most misunderstood parable is that of the Ten Virgins, incorrectly represented as the Church with five virgins rejected for not having the Holy Spirit. How does one "**sell**" and "**buy**" the Holy Spirit, how does one "**trim**" the Holy Spirit, how does one ask another to "**give**" the Holy Spirit? Rather this is acceptance or rejection based on work and faith. The word "Midnight" in the passage below, refers to when the Lord comes back at the end of the age.

*"**Then** (Tribulation and His 2nd coming) shall the **<u>kingdom of heaven</u>** be likened unto **ten virgins**, which took their lamps, and went forth to meet the bridegroom. And five of them were wise, and five were foolish. They that were foolish took their lamps, and took no oil with them: But the*

*wise took oil in their vessels with their lamps. While the bridegroom tarried, they all slumbered and slept. And at **midnight** there was a cry made, **Behold, the bridegroom cometh**; go ye out to meet him. Then all those virgins arose, and **trimmed their lamps**. And the foolish said unto the wise, **Give us of your oil**; for our lamps are gone out. But the wise answered, saying, **Not so; lest there be not enough for us and you: but go ye rather to them that sell, and buy for yourselves**. And while they **went to buy**, the bridegroom came; and **they that were ready went in with him to the marriage**: and the **door was shut**. Afterward came also the other virgins, saying, Lord, Lord, open to us. But he answered and said, Verily I say unto you, **I know you not**. Watch therefore, for ye know neither the day nor the hour wherein the Son of man cometh." Matt 25:1-13*

The 10 virgins represent companions to the bride as the maids of honour for it is their great honour to serve the church. Psalms 45 is a picture of marriage of the bride (Church) to the King. *"Kings' **daughters** were among **thy honourable women**: upon thy **right hand did stand the queen in <u>gold</u> of Ophir**"* Psalms 45:9 The daughter(s) in verse 9 are the Jewish women. The daughter in verse 13 below is the bride.

*"The king's **daughter** is all glorious within: **her clothing is of wrought gold**. She shall be brought unto the king in raiment of needlework: <u>the virgins her companions</u> that follow her shall be brought unto thee. With **gladness and rejoicing shall they be brought**: they shall enter into **the king's palace**." Psalms 45:13-15*

*"Let us be glad and rejoice, and give honour to him: for the **marriage of the Lamb is come**, and his **wife hath made herself ready**. And to her **was <u>granted</u>** (no works) that she should be arrayed in fine linen, clean and white: for the **fine linen is the righteousness** of saints. And he saith unto me, Write, <u>**Blessed**</u> **are they which are** <u>**called**</u> unto the **marriage supper** of the Lamb..." Rev 19:7-9*

Revelation 19 paints a picture of the bride coming with the Bridegroom to be married on earth. From Matthew 22 and 25, that should be clear. The marriage of the Church to the Lamb cannot come until all judgement of the Tribulation is done. In Revelation 19, we see the bride is ready and arrayed in white linen. John is told to write blessed are those **guests/friends called** unto the marriage supper, and by default the wedding. A bride is not "called" to a marriage supper. Jesus will lead the armies in Heaven (bride (church), OT, and Tribulation saints) dressed in fine linen to earth where He will smite the nations at the end of the Tribulation. Those Tribulation survivors found naked **without** a fine linen wedding garment after the sheep and goat judgement begins, are **cast** out (Matt 22:12). Then shall those "armies" rule and reign with Him in the Kingdom of Heaven, *"And hast made us unto our God kings and priests: and* **we shall reign** *on the* **earth"** Rev 5:10

> *"Let us be glad and rejoice, and give honour to him: for* **the marriage of the Lamb is come, and his wife hath made herself ready.** *And to* **her** *was granted that she should be* **arrayed in fine linen, clean and white:** *for the* **fine linen is** *the* **righteousness** *of saints. And he saith unto me, Write,* **Blessed** *are they which* **are called unto the marriage supper of the Lamb.** *And he saith unto me, These are the true sayings of God. And I fell at his feet to worship him. And he said unto me, See thou do it not: I am thy fellowservant, and of thy brethren that have the testimony of Jesus: worship God: for the testimony of Jesus is the spirit of prophecy. And I saw* **heaven opened,** *and* **behold a white horse;** *and he that sat upon him was called Faithful and True, and in righteousness he* **doth judge and make war.** *His eyes were as a flame of fire, and on his head were many crowns; and he had a name written, that no man knew,*

*but he himself. And he was clothed with a vesture dipped in blood: and his name is called The Word of God. And the **armies which were in heaven followed him** upon **white horses,** clothed in **fine linen,** white and clean. And out of his mouth goeth a sharp sword, that with it **he should smite** the **nations:** and he shall rule them with a rod of iron: and **he treadeth the winepress** of the fierceness and **wrath of Almighty God.**" Rev 19:7-15*

By force it was taken the first time, by force it shall be returned to the King. Then shall come the Kingdom of Heaven on Earth.

THE DAY OF CHRIST &
THE DAY OF THE LORD

The second coming of the Lord is understood to occur in two distinct phases. The first phase involves **the Lord gathering believers together to meet Him in the air**. During this event, the faithful receive their spiritual, resurrected bodies. This gathering is commonly known as the **Rapture** and is described as the moment when those who have died in Christ, along with those who are alive in Christ, are united with the Lord above.

The second phase takes place when the Lord returns to Earth in judgment. At this time, He comes to destroy those who oppose Him, often referred to as the heathen. This event is marked by a display of divine authority and the fulfillment of prophetic judgment.

The first phase, the gathering in the air, is associated with the Day of Christ. The term "**Christ**" and what it represents is key, appearing exactly *555* times in the text. The Day of Christ is **distinctly different** from the **Day of the**

Lord, as it refers specifically to the Resurrection, the Rapture, the moment believers are caught up to be with Christ and transformed into their resurrected bodies.

"For the Lord himself shall descend from heaven with a shout, with the voice of the archangel, and with the trump of God: and the dead in **Christ** *shall rise first: Then we which are alive and remain shall be* **caught up together** *with them in the clouds, to* **meet the Lord in the air:** *and so shall we ever be with the Lord." 1 Thess 4:16-17*

"Now we beseech you, brethren, by the coming of our Lord Jesus **Christ,** *and by our* **gathering together unto him,"** *2 Thessalonians 2:1*

"And **hath raised us up together,** *and made us sit together in heavenly places in* **Christ Jesus:** *Ephesians"* *2:6*

Many will say "the Day of Christ" is a mistranslation and should read, "the Day of the Lord", however, the Day of Christ is intentional and accurate. The King James Bible (KJB) is exact and perfect in its definition of language, patterns, and word choices. It serves as its own best interpreter, providing clarity through its internal consistency. This fact of perfection has been proven many times over; however, the church has been programmed by the academics for decades to think one must learn the original translations to fully understand the Word of God. This mindset has contributed to the proliferation of numerous versions and translations, leading to confusion and dilution of the message. One must consider: Why would God expect believers across the world to learn ancient languages to comprehend His Word? Scripture itself affirms, *"For my yoke is **easy**, and my burden is **light**."* Matthew 11:30. Either God is sovereign or He is not. There is one God, one way of Salvation, one Church, and one Word (John 1:1), so why are there so many iterations of each? It is a manifestation of the "mystery of iniquity" at work.

The "**Day of Christ**" is used three times along with two other repetitions that include: "**day** of our Lord Jesus **Christ**", and the "**day** of Jesus **Christ**", for a total of **five** entries; arguably another way to imply the Trinity as 555/5 = 111. Jesus as the "**Christ**" points to His finished work of the cross as a **savior** and for the **victory** of all believers. He died for the forgiveness of our sins and defeated death allowing us to obtain resurrected bodies, eternal life, and **enter** the **Kingdom of God**.

*"Who hath **saved us**, and called us with an **holy calling**, **not** according to our **works**, but according to his own purpose and grace, which was given us in **Christ Jesus before the world began**, But is now **made manifest** by the **appearing** of our **Saviour Jesus Christ**, who hath **abolished***

> *death, and hath brought **life** and **immortality** to light **through** the gospel:"* 2 Tim 1:9-10 (clearly the Day of Christ)

> *"But thanks be to God, which **giveth us** the **victory through** our Lord Jesus **Christ"** 1 Corinthians 15:57.*

> *"For since by man came **death**, by man came also the **resurrection** of the dead. For as in Adam all die, even so in **Christ** shall all be **made alive**. But every man in his own order: **Christ** the firstfruits; afterward they that are **Christ's** at his coming." 1 Corinthians 15:21-23*

> ***"To the end*** *(end of Church age) he may stablish your hearts **unblameable in holiness before God**, even our Father, **at the coming** of our Lord Jesus Christ with all his saints." 1 Thessalonians 3:13*

Jesus will continue His work in us until **that** day. Four of the five entries are shown below: the fifth to show in a latter chapter for a larger discussion.

> *"For God is my record, how greatly I long after you all in the bowels of Jesus Christ. And this I pray, that your love may abound yet more and more in knowledge and in all judgment; That ye may approve things that are excellent; that ye*

*may be **sincere** and **without offence till the** <u>day of Christ</u>;" Phil 1:8-10*

*"That ye may be **blameless and harmless**, the sons of God, **without rebuke**, in the midst of a crooked and perverse nation, among whom ye shine as lights in the world; Holding forth the word of life; that **I may rejoice** in the <u>day of Christ</u>, that I have not run in vain, neither laboured in vain." Phil 2:15-16*

*"That in every thing ye are **enriched** by him, in all utterance, and in all knowledge; Even as the **testimony of Christ** was **confirmed** in you: So that ye come behind in no gift; **waiting for the coming** of our Lord Jesus Christ: Who shall also **confirm you** unto <u>the end</u>,* (Rapture, end of Church age) *that ye may be **blameless** in the <u>day of our Lord Jesus Christ</u>." 1 Cor 1:5-8*

*"For your fellowship in the gospel from the first day until now; Being confident of this very thing, that he which hath **begun a good work** in you **will perform it until** the <u>day of Jesus Christ</u>:" Phil 1:5-6*

In the previous chapter, it was shown that the marriage of the Lamb does not happen until the end of the Tribulation on the earth. Let us not forget we must all stand before the judgement seat of Christ after we are taken up as part of the preparation of the bride (Rev 19:7). Here our works will be judged, and we will receive any crowns we have earned.

Although scripture does not specify the duration of the judgment seat, certain key events will unfold during this period. Believers will witness the opening of the seven-sealed book, an act that marks the commencement of the Tribulation period as described in Revelation 5, and the sealing of the 144,000, detailed in Revelation 7. Do you realize Satan will still have access to Heaven with the Church until the mid-point of the Tribulation? The Church will witness the war in Heaven when Satan is cast out and the execution of many other judgements.

> *"For we must **all appear** before the **judgment seat of Christ**; that every one may receive the things done in his body, according to that he hath done, whether it be **good or bad.**" 2 Corinthians 5:10*

> *"Henceforth there is laid up for me a **crown of righteousness**, which the Lord, the righteous judge, shall give me **at that day** (the Judgment seat of Christ): and not to me only, but unto all them also that love his appearing." 2 Tim 4:8*

> *"My little children, these things write I unto you, that ye sin not. And if any man sin, we have an*

*advocate with the Father, Jesus **Christ** the righ-teous:"* 1 John 2:1

*"For my **sword** shall be **bathed in heaven**: behold, it shall come down upon Idumea, and upon the people of my curse, to judgment."* Isaiah 34:5

*"And there was **war in heaven**: Michael and his angels fought against the dragon; and the dragon fought and his angels, And **prevailed not**; neither was their place found any more in heaven"* Rev 12:7-8.

We will examine one of the most quoted passages in the bible a little later. *"That ye be not soon shaken in mind, or be troubled, neither by spirit, nor by word, nor by letter as from us, as that the **day of__Christ__** is at hand."* 2 Thessalonians 2:2.

The Day of the Lord

The phrase "Day of the Lord" appears exactly **25** times throughout the scriptures, consistently referring to the "time of the end" as described in the Book of Daniel (chapters 8, 11, and 12). This period is marked by Jesus executing judgment upon the earth, administering the most severe judgments during the Tribulation. The Day of the Lord specifically denotes the second half of the Tribulation period, spanning 3.5 years, and culminates in the climactic battle of Armageddon and the "great winepress."

The designation of "**Lord**" refers to Jesus as King and Judge over all the earth. Revelation 19:11-21 expounds on this and verse 16 specifically states, *"And he hath on his vesture and on his thigh a name written, KING OF KINGS, AND LORD OF LORDS"*. John said all judgement has been given to the Son. *"For the Father judgeth no man, but hath committed **all judgment unto the Son:**"* John 5:22. Interestingly, the word "Heathen" is used 150 times and "image" 100 times and both are multiples of 25.

Identifying the midpoint of the Tribulation is key for this book. Jesus addresses when the world will end and discusses the latter half of the Tribulation, known as the Day of the Lord.

*"And this **gospel of the kingdom** (of Heaven) shall be **preached in all the world** for a witness unto all nations; **and <u>then</u> shall the end come.** When ye therefore **shall see the abomination of desolation,** (AC) spoken of by Daniel the prophet, **stand in the holy place,** (whoso readeth, let him understand:) Then let them which be in Judaea flee into the mountains:* (Rev 12:14) *Let him which is on the housetop not come down to take any thing out of his house: Neither let him which is in the field return back to take his clothes. And woe unto them that are with child, and to them that give suck in those days! But **pray** ye that **your***

flight (Rev 12:14) **be not** *in the winter,* **neither on the sabbath day:** (law/commandments of God have returned) **For <u>then</u>** *shall be* <u>**great**</u> **tribulation,** *such as was not since the beginning of the world to this time, no, nor ever shall be. And except those days should be shortened, there should no flesh be saved: but for the* **elect's sake** (Jews) *those days shall be shortened. Then if any man shall say unto you, Lo,* **here is Christ,** *or there; believe it not. For there shall arise* **false Christs,** *and* **false prophets,** *and shall shew great signs and wonders; insomuch that, if it were possible, they shall deceive the* **very elect.** (Jews) *Behold, I have told you before. Wherefore if they shall say unto you, Behold, he is in the desert; go not forth: behold, he is* **in the secret chambers;** (possibly the AC (acting as Christ) in the chambers of the Ark of Covenant, *Ez 7:22) believe it not. For as the* **lightning cometh** *out of the east, and shineth even unto the west;* (this is the Rapture that will be seen) **so shall <u>also</u> the coming** (just before the very end) *of the* **Son of man be.** *For wheresoever the* **carcase** *is,* (dead bodies from the Harvest/winepress at the very end) *there will the eagles be gathered together." (Rev 19:17) Matt 24:14-28*

The coming "great winepress" will perhaps be the most dramatic event in the history of this current world. It is the time when the Lord and two of His angels will "reap" the "harvest" of heathen that come to fight against Him in a place called Armageddon (Rev 16:16). The blood from that harvest will form a river some 200 miles long and about five feet deep, an unimaginable slaughter of the heathen (Rev 14:14-20)

Isaiah 34 and part of Joel 3 provide another perspective on the Day of the Lord. Some excerpts are included here.

*"For the **indignation of the LORD** is upon **all nations**, and his **fury** upon **all their armies:** he hath utterly **destroyed them,** he hath **delivered them to the slaughter.** (great winepress) Their slain also shall be cast out, and their stink shall come up out of their **carcases,** (Matt 24:28) and the **mountains shall be melted with their blood.** (Rev 14:20) And **all the host of heaven shall be dissolved,** (2 Peter 3:10-12) and the **heavens shall be rolled together as a scroll:** (rev 6:14) (back to their original state from creation) and **all their host** (angels) **shall fall down,** (Rev 6:13) as the leaf falleth off from the vine, and as a falling fig from the fig tree. For my **sword** shall be **bathed in heaven:** (war in Heaven, Rev 12:7) behold,*

*it shall come down upon **Idumea**, and upon the people of my curse, **to judgment**." Is 34:2-5 (see Ez 36:1-7, 35:14-15, Idumea refers to Heathen, split of Jacob & Esau)*

*"Proclaim ye this among the **Gentiles**; Prepare war, wake up the mighty men, let all the men of war draw near; let them come up: Beat your plow-shares into swords, and your pruninghooks into spears: let the weak say, I am strong. **Assemble yourselves**, and come, **all ye heathen**, and gather yourselves together round about: thither cause thy **mighty ones** (angels) to **come down**, O LORD. Let the **heathen be wakened**, and come up to the **valley of Jehoshaphat**: (Armageddon) for there will I sit to **judge all the heathen** round about. Put ye in the **sickle**, for the **harvest is ripe**: come, get you down; for the press is full, the fats over-flow; for their wickedness is great Multitudes, multitudes in the **valley of decision**: for the **day of the LORD** is near in the valley of decision. Joel 3:9-14*

The 7-year Tribulation will fulfill the wrath of God against the heathen and bring a remnant of Israel back unto Him. The people that physically survive the seven years until the end, including the great winepress harvest and the sheep and goat judgement, will be saved and granted entrance into the Kingdom of Heaven. *"And ye shall be hated of all men for my name's sake: but he that **endureth to the end** shall be **saved"** Matthew 10:22.* Now that the Kingdom of Heaven has been explained previously, this passage will be understood.

*"Another parable spake he unto them; The **king-dom of heaven** is like unto leaven, which a woman took, and hid in three measures of meal, till the whole was leavened... ...and his disciples came unto him, saying, Declare unto us the parable of the tares of the field. He answered and said unto them, He that soweth the good seed is the **Son of man;*** (Jesus) *The field is the world; the good seed are the children of the **kingdom;*** (of Heaven) *but the **tares*** (heathen) *are the **children of the wicked one*** (AC); *The enemy that sowed them is the **devil;** the **harvest*** (great winepress) *is the end of the world; and the **reapers are the angels.** As therefore the tares are gathered and burned in the fire; so shall it be in the end of this world. The Son of man shall **send forth his angels,** and they shall **gather out*** (Matt 25:32) *of **his kingdom*** (of Heaven) *all things that offend, and them which do iniquity; And shall cast them into a furnace of fire: there shall be wailing and gnashing of teeth.* (Matt 25:41) *Then shall the righteous shine forth*

as the sun in the kingdom of their Father. Who hath ears to hear, let him hear." Matt 13:33-43

"For the day is near, even the **day of the LORD** *is near, a cloudy day; it shall be the time of the* **heathen.***"* Ezekiel 30:3

"For the **day of the LORD** *is near upon all the* **heathen:** *as thou hast done, it shall be done unto thee: thy reward shall return upon thine own head."* Obadiah 1:15

THE FOUR PHASES OF THE GOSPEL

There is only one Gospel (Gal 1:8) however, that one Gospel has four different phases spoken within the New Testament. All four are comprised by the shed blood of Christ. Two for the Church age and two for the Tribulation period. "Gospel" means "Good News". Each has a place within its respective categories. The biblical number four represents a wholeness in structure or nature like the four points of the cross, the four seasons on earth, the four states of physical matter, the four letters of DNA and the four chambers of the human heart.

- The Gospel of the Grace of God » The Kingdom of God
- The Glorious Gospel » The Day of Christ Church age ↑ Tribulation period ↓
- The Gospel of the Kingdom » The Kingdom of Heaven
- The Everlasting Gospel » The Day of the Lord

All four have one aspect in common: **Fear God** used ten times in the text from Genesis to Revelation. Ten is the number of the whole unit, the complete measure of something like the ten plagues of Egypt and the ten commandments.

*"And Joseph said unto them the third day, This do, and live; for I **fear God**:" Gen 42:18*

*"Saying with a loud voice, **Fear God**, and give glory to him; for the hour of his judgment is come: and worship him that made heaven, and earth, and the sea, and the fountains of waters." Rev 14:7*

*"And a voice came out of the throne, saying, Praise our God, **all ye his servants**, and **ye that fear him**, both small and great." Rev 19:5*

We will examine each gospel that corresponds with the two Kingdoms and the two Days. It is important to demonstrate each "gospel" for proper interpretation. Perhaps the gospel most are familiar with is the first and current Salvation **"Gospel of Christ"**. There are seven worded variations of this gospel with 24 entries or 4 x 6. Six, the number for mankind. The variations are as follows:

- Gospel of God x 7
- Gospel of Jesus Christ x 1
- Gospel of the **Grace** of God x 1
- Gospel of His Son x 1

- Gospel of Christ x 11
- Gospel of Peace x 2
- Gospel of our Lord Jesus Christ x 1

This gospel corresponds with the Kingdom of God. It is for the Church age only, ending at the Rapture. To obtain a spiritual body and enter the Kingdom of God, one must *"…confess with thy mouth the Lord Jesus, and shalt believe in thine heart that God hath raised him from the dead, thou shalt be saved"* Romans 10:9. There are no **"works"** involved. It is by **grace** and **faith** one is saved. *"For **by grace are ye saved through faith**; and that not of yourselves: it is the gift of God:"* Ephesians 2:8. Faith can be defined as confidence or trust in the authority of God's Word.

The next gospel is the **"Glorious Gospel"** residing within the framework of the **"Day of Christ"** and denotes His **"Glorious Appearing"**, understood as the initial stage of His Second Coming. At this time, He will gather all believers and <u>usher them into</u> the **Kingdom of God.**

*"According to the **glorious gospel** of the **blessed God, which was committed to my trust. And I thank Christ Jesus our Lord, who hath enabled me,** for that he counted me faithful, putting me into the ministry;"* 1 Timothy 1:11-12

"But if our gospel be hid, it is hid to them that are lost: In whom the god of this world hath blinded the minds of them which believe not, lest the light

*of the **glorious gospel** of **Christ**, who is the image of God, should shine unto them. For we preach not ourselves, but Christ Jesus the Lord; and ourselves your servants for Jesus' sake."* 2 Cor 4:3-5

*"That the trial of your faith, being much more precious than of gold that perisheth, though it be tried with fire, might be found unto praise and honour and **glory** at the **appearing** of Jesus **Christ:**"* 1 Peter 1:7

*"Looking for that **blessed** hope, and the **glorious appearing** of the great God and our Saviour Jesus **Christ;** Who gave himself for us, that he might **redeem us** from **all iniquity**, and **purify unto himself** a peculiar people, zealous of good works."* Titus 2:13-14

The Glorious Gospel is the "blessed hope" of all watchful Christians "waiting" to be changed.

*"And not only they, but ourselves also, which have the firstfruits of the Spirit, even we ourselves **groan** within ourselves, **waiting** for the adoption, to wit, the **redemption** of our **body**"* Romans 8:23

*"And the Lord direct your hearts into the love of God, and into the **patient waiting** for **Christ**"* 2 Thessalonians 3:5

Next is the **"Gospel of the Kingdom"** that will include the "testimony of Jesus" and includes "works" and "faith", outlined in the Kingdom of Heaven parables of Matthew. It emphasizes the coming Lordship and rule of Jesus on Earth. The martyred **Jewish** and **gentile** Tribulation **saints,** those that die refusing the mark of the beast, will enter into the Kingdom of God (resurrected spiritual body) to join the Church and OT saints in the Kingdom of God, while the living Jewish **remnant** saved at the end of the Tribulation will enter into the Kingdom of Heaven by keeping the **commandments** of God and the **faith/testimony** (includes the Gospel of the Kingdom message) of Jesus. *"… for the testimony of Jesus is the* **spirit of prophecy**" Rev 19:10.

> *"And the dragon was wroth with the woman, and went to make war with the* **<u>remnant</u>** *of her seed, which* **keep the commandments** *of* **God,** *and have the* **testimony of Jesus Christ.**" *Revelation 12:17*

> *"Here is the patience* **of the <u>saints</u>:** *here are they that* **keep the commandments** *of* **God,** *and the* **faith** *of Jesus."* *Revelation 14:12*

Survivors from the rest of the nations, referred to as the gentiles, will face entrance to the Kingdom based on what is commonly called the "sheep and goat" judgment. In this judgment, their righteousness is undeniably determined by their "works". These gentile survivors are also required to maintain the faith and testimony of Jesus that was preached to them by the 144,000 during this period.

It is very possible Jesus is speaking directly of the 144,000 virgins as "my brethren", rather than the Jewish people in general in the following verse, for the 144,000 will traverse the entire globe during the first half of the Tribulation. *"And the King shall answer and say unto them, Verily I say unto you, Inasmuch as ye have done it unto one of the least of these **my brethren**, ye have **done** it **unto me**"* Matt 25:40. Read all of Matthew 25:31-46 for context.

Jesus said the *"gospel of the Kingdom"* will be preached again during the Tribulation for **all nations.** *"And this **gospel of the kingdom** shall be preached in all the world for a witness unto **all nations**; and* <u>*then*</u> *shall the end come"* Mat 24:14. *"And in the days of these kings shall the **God of heaven** <u>**set up**</u> **a kingdom,** which shall never be destroyed: and the kingdom shall not be left to other people, but it shall break in pieces and **consume all these kingdoms,** and it shall **stand for ever.**"* Daniel 2:44.

The Antichrist will not take to kindly to this gospel as it means the end for his kingdom. During the last half of the Tribulation, after that gospel has been preached to all the world, *"And **he (AC) shall speak great words** against the most High, and shall **wear out the saints** (die as martyrs) of the most High, and think to **change times and laws:** and they **shall be given into his hand** until a time and* *times and the dividing of time."* Daniel 7:25.

The **law and sacrifices** will continue throughout the Millennial Reign. Ezekiel chapters 43-45 provide the details of a yet future Temple with instructions given by the Lord. This Temple will be built after the Tribulation but **before** the beginning of the Millennial Reign for the "last days" are not part of the Millennium.

> *"And it shall come to pass **in the <u>last days</u>,** that the mountain of the **LORD'S house shall be established** in the top of the mountains, and shall be exalted above the hills; and **all nations shall flow unto it.** And many people shall go and say, Come ye, and let us go up to the mountain of the LORD, to the house of the God of Jacob; and he will teach us of his ways, and we will walk in his paths: for **out of Zion shall <u>go forth the law</u>,** and the **word of the LORD** from Jerusalem"* Is 2:2-3.

In this Temple, various sacrifices will be made including the yearly burnt offering for the sin of the Nation of Israel by the Prince. It is not known who this Prince will be. *"And upon that day shall the **prince** prepare for himself and for all the people of the land a bullock for a **sin offering"*** Ezekiel 45:22.

> *"**All the people of the land** shall give this oblation for the **prince** in Israel. And it shall be the prince's part to give **burnt offerings,** and **meat offerings,***

*and **drink offerings**, in the feasts, and in the **new moons**, and in the **sabbaths**, in all solemnities of the house of Israel: he shall prepare the **sin offering**, and the meat offering, and **the burnt offering**, and the peace offerings, to <u>make reconciliation</u> for the house of Israel"* Ez 45:16-17.

*And it shall come to pass, that **every one that is left of all the nations which came against Jerusalem** shall even go up from **year to year** to worship **the King**, the LORD of hosts, and to **keep the feast of tabernacles**. And it shall be, that whoso will not come up of all the families of the earth unto Jerusalem to worship the King, the LORD of hosts, even upon them shall be no rain.* Zec 14:16-17

The final Gospel is the **"Everlasting Gospel"**, used once in the book of Revelation. It is the "good news" and encouragement to those survivors who have kept their allegiance to God during the first half of Tribulation, that His final judgements are about to commence on the earth, and their time of suffering will soon come to an end. It is the clarification that He is sovereign, and His authority is complete and final. Fear God, worship God.

*"And I saw another angel fly in the midst of heaven, having the **everlasting gospel** to preach **unto them that dwell on the earth, and to every***

*nation, and kindred, and tongue, and people, Saying with a loud voice, **Fear God, and give glory to him;** for the **hour of his judgment is come:** and **worship him that made heaven, and earth,** and the sea, and the fountains of waters."* Rev 14:6-7

*"And I fell at his feet to worship him. And he said unto me, See thou do it not: I am thy fellowservant, and of thy brethren that **have the testimony of Jesus: worship God:** for the **testimony of Jesus** is the **spirit of prophecy."** Rev 19:10* (the messenger speaking to John just before the "great winepress" is to commence)

Some have suggested the Rapture may take place years before the beginning of the Tribulation, however that seems illogical and out of character for there would be nobody left to preach a certain gospel/deliverance during that time. Perhaps it is no more than a year at the most between the Rapture and beginning of the Tribulation. Perhaps even just a day as Luke 17 suggests.

*"Likewise also as it was in the days of Lot; they did eat, they drank, they bought, they sold, they planted, they builded; But the <u>same day</u> that Lot **went out** of Sodom **it rained fire and brimstone** from heaven, and destroyed them all." Luke 17:28-29*

*"The Lord **knoweth how to deliver the godly out** of temptations, and to **reserve the unjust** unto the **day of judgment** to be punished:"* 2 Peter 2:9

In the end, the remnant of the nation of Israel for all their sins shall be saved:

*"Behold, the days come, saith the LORD, that I will make a **new covenant with the house of Israel, and with the house of Judah:** Not according to the covenant that I made with their fathers in the day that I took them by the hand to bring them out of the land of Egypt; which my covenant **they brake,** although **I was an husband unto them,** saith the LORD: But this shall be the covenant that I will make with the <u>house of Israel</u>; After those days, saith the LORD, I will **put my law in their inward parts, and write it in their hearts;** and will be their God, and they shall be my people."* Jer 31:31-33

*"Verily thou art a God that **hidest thyself,** O God of Israel, the **Saviour.** They shall be ashamed, and also confounded, all of them: they shall **go to confusion together that are makers of idols. But Israel shall be saved in the LORD with an everlasting salvation:** ye shall not be ashamed nor confounded world without end."* Is 45:15-17

THE 144,000 &
THE TWO WITNESSES

The ministry of Jesus lasted between 3 to 3.5 years and focused on the land of Israel with a 150 mile north to south diameter; traveling mostly on foot. During the Tribulation, a special group of men known as the 144,000 virgins, special in the sense they are tightly tied to Him, will evangelize the entire world within a 3 to 3.5 period from sometime after the beginning until they are all martyred by the time of the fifth seal, just before the mid-point of the Tribulation. Most agree Moses and Elijah will be the two witnesses during this time representing the law (judge, Rom 2:12) and the prophets. The 144,000 can be seen as priest to complete an image of the Old Testament period representing Jesus as He is also a priest, a prophet, and judge (Heb 2:17, Rev 19:10, John 5:22). The 144,000 will **declare** and preach the "testimony of Jesus **Christ**".

*"And the dragon was wroth with the woman, and went to make war with the **remnant** of her seed,*

which keep the commandments of God, and have the testimony of Jesus Christ." Rev 12:17

Let us surmise as to why these men are so special. We know for certain they are 12,000 men from 12 Tribes of Israel (Rev 7), but they are also called the *"firstfruits unto God and to the Lamb"*, *"virgins"*, *"in their mouth was found no guile"*, and *"without fault before the throne of God"* (Rev 14:4-5) These statements seem to outline something that would be impossible for men living on earth. Jesus never married, so by default He was a virgin. Notice the word "firstfruits" is plural below in 1 Corinthians. Why is it plural and not singular? It matches the "firstfruits" of Revelation 14 which we will look at shortly.

> *"For even hereunto were ye called: because* **Christ** *also suffered for us, leaving us an example, that ye should follow his steps: Who did* **no sin, neither was guile found** *in his* **mouth:** *"* 1 Peter 2:21-22

> *"Pilate saith unto him,* **What is truth?** *And when he had said this, he went out again unto the Jews, and saith unto them, I find in him* **no fault at all.** *"* John 18:38

> *"But now is Christ risen from the dead, and become the* **firstfruits** *of them that slept. For since by man came death, by man came also the resurrection of the dead. For as in Adam all die,*

*even so in Christ shall all be made alive. But every man in his own order: Christ the **firstfruits**; afterward they that are Christ's at his coming." 1 Cor 15:20-23*

Not to say that it is impossible for God, but how hard would it be today to find 12,000 virgin men meeting this description from Israel today? Isaiah 53 is a prophetic outline of Jesus Christ and His death on the cross for the redemption of mankind. An interesting statement is made in that chapter, *"He was taken from prison and from judgment: and <u>who shall declare his generation</u>? for **he was <u>cut off</u>** out of the land of the living: for the transgression of my people was he stricken"* Is 53:8.

At the time of the birth of Jesus, all male babies from newborn to the age of about two were killed by King Herod, wiping out an entire generation of brotherly, male children that could have ***declared*** and ***<u>revealed</u>*** Jesus to the Jewish people at the time of His ministry possibly resulting in a different outcome of the Jews accepting the Kingdom of Heaven at the time. *"Then Herod, when he saw that he was mocked of the wise men, was exceeding wroth, and sent forth, **and slew all the children** that were in **Bethlehem**, and **in all the coasts thereof,** from **two years old and under,** according to the time which he had diligently enquired of the wise men"* Matt 2:16. The "coasts thereof" includes all of Israel, *"And the LORD spake unto*

Moses, saying, Command the children of Israel, and say unto them, When ye come into the land of Canaan; (this is the land that shall fall unto you for an inheritance, even the **land of Canaan** *with the* **coasts thereof:)**" Numbers 34:2

Continuing in the next couple of verses in Matthew two, a prophesy is mentioned to be fulfilled, *"Then* **was fulfilled** *that which was spoken by Jeremy the prophet, saying, In* **Rama** *was there a voice heard,* **lamentation, and weeping,** *and great mourning,* **Rachel weeping** *for* **her children,** *and would not be comforted,* **because they are not**" *Matt 2:17-18*. Here is the prophecy when it was spoken in Jeremiah chapter 31.

> *"Thus saith the LORD; A voice was heard in* **Ramah, lamentation,** *and bitter* **weeping;** *Rahel* **weeping for her children** *refused to be comforted for her children, because* **they were not.** *Thus saith the LORD;* **Refrain** *thy voice* **from weeping,** *and thine eyes from tears: for thy work shall be* **rewarded,** *saith the LORD; and they shall <u>come again</u> from the land of the enemy. And there is <u>hope in thine end</u>, saith the LORD, that thy children* **<u>shall come again to their own border</u>**." *Jer 31:15-17*

Rachel was one of the wives of Jacob and gave birth to Joseph and Benjamin. Joseph, in Christian biblical interpretation and theology, is often seen as a type, as a typological foreshadowing of the key aspects of Jesus' life, ministry, suffering, exaltation, and saving work.

Benjamin, as an infant, was **separated from his brother** Joseph when he was sold into slavery. Joeph would have been around 17 at the time. After Joseph came to power in Egypt, he **revealed himself** to his brothers and he wept first with Benjamin (Gen 45:14)

Jeremiah chapter 31 also speaks of the restoration of Israel and a time when God will make a new covenant with Israel and put His law in their hearts (Jer 31:31-34).

*At the same time, saith the LORD, **will I be the God** of all the **families of Israel, and they shall be my people.** Thus saith the LORD, The people which were left of the sword **found grace in the wilderness;** even Israel, when I went to cause him to rest. Jer 31:1-2*

Just before the 144,000 are marked in their forehead with the seal of the living God, "the Father's name", the angels are seen holding back the four winds of the earth. For what purpose are they holding back the winds? Is this when the prophecy for the Vally of the Dry Bones is fulfilled? The 12,000 from each tribe represents the "whole house of Israel".

*"And after these things I saw four angels standing on the four corners of the earth, **holding the***

<u>four winds</u> *of the earth, that **the wind should not blow** on the earth, nor on the sea, nor on any tree. And I saw another angel ascending from the east, having **the seal of the living God**: and he cried with a loud voice to the four angels, to whom it was given to hurt the earth and the sea, Saying, Hurt not the earth, neither the sea, nor the trees, **till we have sealed the servants** of our God in their foreheads." Rev 7:1-4*

*"The hand of the LORD was upon me, and carried me out in the spirit of the LORD, and set me down in the midst of the valley which was full of bones, And caused me to pass by them round about: and, behold, there were very many in the open valley; and, lo, they were very dry. And he said unto me, Son of man, can these bones live? And I answered, O Lord GOD, thou knowest. Again he said unto me, Prophesy upon these bones, and say unto them, O ye dry bones, hear the word of the LORD. Thus saith the Lord GOD unto these bones; Behold, **I will cause breath to enter into you, and ye shall live:** And I will lay sinews upon you, and will bring up flesh upon you, and cover you with skin, and put breath in you, and ye shall live; and **ye shall know that I am the LORD.** So I prophesied as I*

was commanded: and as I prophesied, there was a noise, and behold a shaking, and the bones came together, bone to his bone. And when I beheld, lo, the sinews and the flesh came up upon them, and the skin covered them above: **but there was no breath in them.** *Then said he unto me,* **Prophesy unto the wind,** *prophesy, son of man, and say to the wind, Thus saith the Lord GOD;* **Come from the <u>four winds,</u> O breath,** *and breathe upon these <u>slain,</u> that* **they may <u>live</u>.** *So I prophesied as he commanded me, and the breath came into them,* **and they lived,** *and stood up upon their feet, an* **exceeding great army.**" *Ex 37:1-10 (see Rev 19:9 for "army")*

"Then he said unto me, Son of man, these bones are the **whole house of Israel**: *behold, they say, Our bones are dried, and our hope is lost: we are <u>cut off</u> for our parts."* Ez 37:11

Jesus was also prophesied to be "cut off", *"He was taken from prison and from judgment: and who shall declare his generation? for he was* **cut off out of the land of the living:** *for the transgression of my people was he stricken."* Isaiah 53:8

Now let us look at the entire passage in Revelation 14. This passage is after the 144,000 have all been martyred and are standing before the throne of God. Keep in mind that only Jesus **came** in His Father's name. How is it that the 144,000 are able to come as witnesses with the Father's name unless they have been set aside for this special mission? *"I am come in my **Father's name,** and ye receive me not: if **another** (AC) shall come in his own name, **him ye will receive.**"* John 5:43

> *"And I looked, and, lo, a Lamb stood on the mount Sion, and with him an **hundred forty and four thousand,** having his **Father's name** (who* knows it other than Jesus) *written in their fore-heads. And I heard a voice from heaven, as the voice of many waters, and as the voice of a great thunder: and I heard the voice of harpers harping with their harps: And they **sung** as it were a **new song before the throne,** and before the four beasts, and the elders: and **no man could learn that song*** (because of their unique circumstances) ***but the hundred and forty and four thousand,** which were **redeemed from the earth.** These are they which were **not defiled with women;** for they are **virgins.** These are they which **follow the Lamb whithersoever he goeth*** (from His resurrection He took them with Him). *These **were redeemed** from **among men*** (their death by Herod's cronies at two and under), ***being the firstfruits*** (resurrected with Jesus) *unto **God** and to the **Lamb.** And in their*

*mouth was found **no guile**: for they are **without fault before the throne of God**. And I saw another angel fly in the midst of heaven, having **the everlasting gospel*** (this gospel preached in the last half as the ministry of the 144,000 is now complete) *to preach unto them that dwell on the earth, and to **every nation, and kindred, and tongue, and people**, Saying with a loud voice, Fear God, and give glory to him; for the **hour of his judgment is come*** (Day of the Lord): *and worship him that made heaven, and earth, and the sea, and the fountains of waters." Rev 14:1-7*

The army of 144,000, all martyred for their witness and their testimony, are seen as souls without a body by John under the **altar** in Heaven at the time of the fifth seal. Their dead bodies are then "raptured out" at the same time as the two witnesses, **the mid-point** of the Tribulation, and are given white robes as seen before the **throne** of God in Revelation 14 above.

*"And when he had opened the **fifth seal**, I saw **under** the altar the **souls*** (not yet resurrected) *of them that were **slain for the word of God**, and **for the testimony which they held**: And they cried with a loud voice, saying, How long, O Lord, holy and true, **dost thou not judge and avenge our blood** on them that dwell on the earth? And*

__white robes__ were __given__ unto every one of them; (now resurrected) *and it was said unto them, that they __should rest yet for a little season__* (rest for the last half of Tribulation until the harvest is reaped of the heathen, Rev 14:15-20) *until their __fellows-ervants__* (gentiles) *also and their __brethren__* (Jews), *that should be __killed as they were__* (beheaded), *should be fulfilled." Rev 6:9-11*

"And I saw thrones, and they sat upon them, and judgment was given unto them: and I saw the __souls of them that were__ __beheaded__ __for the__ __witness of Jesus__, and __for the word of God__, and which had not worshipped the beast, neither his image, neither had received his mark upon their foreheads, or in their hands; and they lived and reigned with Christ a thousand years." Revelation 20:4 (these are the Jewish and gentile saints that __received__ and __believed__ the __truth__ from the 144,000 and then killed for their testimony of Jesus; resurrected at the end of the Tribulation)

Once the 144,000 are sealed with the Father's name in Revelation 7, verse nine shifts ahead in time, nearing the end of the Tribulation, to reveal the result of the 144,000's work (like Revelation 20:4). On a side note, the term "four and twenty elders" in Revelation appears six times, the number for man. In each instance they are the witnesses of the NT Church (12 Apostles, Matt 19:28, Luke 22:30, Rev 21:14) and the OT saints (12 Princes, Num 1:16,44, Rev 21:12) standing before God. Only a select few OT saints, including those twelve princes, were resurrected *after* Jesus & His Firstfruits (Matt 27:52-53), while the remaining OT saints will be resurrected at the end of the Tribulation (Dan 12:1-2) along with the Tribulation saints mentioned in the next passage. In this passage, it is just "elders", but the meaning is the same. Notice speaking of these Tribulation saints, they had to wash their own robes (works) vs the 144,000 that were "given" white robes (Rev 6:11).

> *"**After this** I beheld, and, lo, **a great multitude, which no man could number,** of all nations, and **kindreds, and people, and tongues, stood before the throne,** and before the Lamb, **clothed with white robes,** and palms in their hands; And cried with a loud voice, saying, **Salvation to our God** which sitteth upon the throne, and unto the Lamb. And **all the angels** stood round about the throne, and **about the elders** and the **four beasts,** and fell before the throne on their faces, and worshipped God, **Saying, Amen** (in agreeance with those that just came out of the Tribulation for their Salvation): **Blessing,** and **glory,** and **wisdom,** and **thanksgiving,** and **honour,** and **power,** and **might,** be unto our God for ever and ever. **Amen.** And*

*one of the elders answered, saying unto me, **What are these which are arrayed in white robes? and** whence came they? And I said unto him, Sir, thou knowest. And he said to me, These are they which **came out of great tribulation,** and have <u>washed their robes</u>, and **made them white in the <u>blood</u>** of the Lamb." Rev 7:9-14*

The 144,000 with the Father's name as a seal, will witness on earth in a miraculous way by the **power** of the <u>Holy Ghost</u> so there is no question that by the shed **blood of Jesus** over 2,000 years ago, is what saves a soul from Hell. Chapter six will elaborate.

*"This is he that came by water and blood, even Jesus Christ; not by water only, but by water and blood. And it is the **Spirit that beareth witness,** because the **Spirit is <u>truth</u>**." 1 John 5:6*

*"If we receive the witness of men, **the witness of God is greater:** for this is the witness of God which **he hath testified of his Son**." 1 John 5:9*

*"...These are they which **came out of great trib-ulation,** and have **washed** their robes, and made them white **in the <u>blood</u>** of the **Lamb**." Rev 7:14*

*"And they **overcame** him **by** the <u>blood</u> of the Lamb, and by the **word** of their **testimony;** and*

they loved not their lives unto the death." Rev 12:11

After the Millennial Reign, there will come a time when every saved soul is given the Father's name. *"And there shall be no more curse: but the throne of God and of the Lamb shall be in it; and **his servants** shall serve him: And they shall see his face; and **his name shall be in their foreheads**." Rev 22:3-4*

The Two Witnesses

Moses and Elijah will come before the Day of the Lord to preach the Kingdom of Heaven and the commandments of the law. The Kingdom Gospel from Elijah will be shared with all nations and peoples, while the commandments given by Moses will continue to be followed by Jewish people living around the world. The actions of gentiles are evaluated according to how they treated Jewish people globally during the Tribulation, as described in the Sheep and Goat Judgment from the book of Matthew. The Jewish people that survive are gathered by the angels at the end of the Tribulation and brought to Israel. This is not a rapture/resurrection, but a physical gathering to bring all Jewish people back into the land God gave to them where they remain forever more. At this writing, half (eight million) of the Jewish people still live outside the state of Israel.

"For, behold, the day cometh, that **shall burn as an oven;** *and all the proud, yea, and* **all that do wickedly, shall be stubble:** *and the day that cometh shall burn them up, saith the* LORD *of hosts, that it shall* **leave them** *(the heathen)* **neither root nor branch.** *But unto you that* **fear my name** *shall the Sun of righteousness arise with healing in his wings; and ye shall go forth, and grow up as calves of the stall. And ye shall tread down the wicked; for they shall be ashes under the soles of your feet in the day that I shall do this, saith the* LORD *of hosts.* **Remember ye the law of Moses my servant,** *which I commanded unto him in Horeb for all Israel, with the* **statutes and judgments.** *Behold, I will* **send you Elijah the prophet before the coming of the great and dreadful day of the** LORD: *And he shall turn the heart of the fathers to the children, and the heart of the children to their fathers, lest I come and smite the earth with a curse. "* Malachi 4

*"***Immediately** *after* **the tribulation** *of those days shall the sun be darkened, and the moon shall not give her light, and the stars shall fall from heaven, and the powers of the heavens shall be shaken: And then shall appear the sign of the Son of man in heaven: and then shall all the tribes of*

*the earth mourn, and they shall **see the Son of man coming** in the clouds of heaven with power and great glory. And he shall **send his angels** with a great sound of a trumpet, and they shall **gather together his elect** from the four winds, from one end of heaven to the other."* Matt 24:29-31 (see Ez 36:21-28, Jer 23:1-8, Jer 32:37-41)

Just as Jesus prophesied, *"And this **gospel of the <u>kingdom</u>** shall be preached in **all the world for a witness** unto **all nations;** and <u>**then**</u> **shall the end come"*** Mat 24:14. Had the Jewish people accepted the Kingdom of Heaven the first time Jesus came, Elijah's mission would have been completed. At the transfiguration of Jesus, Moses and Elijah were seen talking to Him.

*"And, behold, there appeared unto them **Moses and Elias** talking with **him.** Then answered Peter, and said unto Jesus, Lord, it is good for us to be here: if thou wilt, let us make here three tabernacles; one for thee, and one for Moses, and one for Elias."* Matt 17:3-4

*"And his disciples asked him, saying, **Why then say the scribes that Elias must first come?** And Jesus answered and said unto them, **Elias truly shall first come, and restore all things.** But I say unto you, That **Elias is come already, and they***

*knew him not, but have done unto him whatso-ever they listed. Likewise shall also the Son of man suffer of them. Then **the disciples understood that he spake unto them of John the Baptist.**"*
Matt 17:10-13

The two witnesses will come **before** the Day of the Lord as we saw in Malachi 4 and prophesy for a 3.5-year period and will be killed by the Antichrist at the mid-point of the Tribulation. The two witnesses will have the power to kill, *"And if any man will **hurt them, fire proceedeth** out of their mouth, and **devoureth their enemies**: and if any man will hurt them, **he must in this manner be killed.**"* *Rev 11:5*. It is very possible the two witnesses are the ones that kill the **"man of sin"** just prior to the mid-point. The 144,000 virgins will be a threat to the AC and his plan to take over the world with their message and conceivably even more so the two witnesses, as they have the power of fire to kill. Perhaps it is the fire of their mouth that withers the Antichrist' right arm and darkens his eye killing him. After the Antichrist is killed, he will rise from the bottomless pit as the "son of perdition" and "continue" "forty and two months" the last half of the Tribulation. The entire world will see this happening on TV and social media in Jerusalem.

*"And I saw one of his heads as it were **wounded to death; and his deadly wound was healed: and***

all the <u>world</u> wondered (saw him rise from the dead) after the beast. And they worshipped the dragon which gave power unto the beast: and they worshipped the beast, saying, Who is like unto the beast? who is able to <u>make war</u> with him? (two witnesses allowed to overpower him until the AC returns from bottomless pit) And there was given unto him a mouth speaking great things and blasphemies; and power was given unto him to <u>continue</u> forty and two months." Rev 13:3-5

"The beast that thou sawest was, and is not; and shall ascend out of the bottomless pit, and go into perdition: and they that dwell on the earth shall <u>wonder</u>, whose names were not written in the book of life from the foundation of the world, when they <u>behold</u> the beast that was, and is not, and yet is." Rev 17:17

"And the LORD said unto me, Take unto thee yet the instruments of a foolish shepherd. For, lo, I will raise up a shepherd in the land, which shall not visit those that be cut off, neither shall seek the young one, nor heal that that is broken, nor feed that that standeth still: but he shall eat the flesh of the fat, and tear their claws in pieces. Woe to the idol shepherd that <u>leaveth the flock</u>! the

sword shall be upon his arm, and upon his right eye: his arm shall be clean dried up, and his right eye shall be utterly darkened." Zec 11:15-17

Shortly after ascending from the bottomless pit, the Antichrist will kill the two witnesses. Their bodies will lie in the streets of Jerusalem for all the world to see and the people will *rejoice* that the Antichrist has killed them for the beast was and now is *"...when they <u>behold</u> the beast that was, and is not, and yet is."* Revelation 17:8

*"And when they shall have finished their testimony, the **beast that <u>ascendeth</u>** (this is the mid-point) **out of the bottomless pit shall make war against them,** and shall overcome them, and **kill them.** And their **dead bodies shall lie in the street** of the **great city,** which spiritually is called Sodom and Egypt, **where** also our Lord was crucified. And they of the people and kindreds and tongues and **nations shall see their dead bodies** three days and an half, and shall not suffer their dead bodies to be put in graves. And they that dwell upon the earth shall rejoice over them, and make merry, and shall send gifts one to another; because these **two prophets tormented them** that dwelt on the earth. And after **three days and an half** (time Jesus was in the tomb) the **Spirit of life** from God entered into them,*

*and **they stood upon their feet**; and great fear fell upon them which saw them. And they heard a great voice from heaven saying unto them, **Come up hither.*** (martyred 144,00 go with them) *And they **ascended up to heaven** in a cloud; and their enemies beheld them." Rev 11:7-12*

The term Antichrist is the general term for the man that causes destruction during the 7-year Tribulation; however, the text makes it clear there is a distinction between the first and second half of the Tribulation in his name, vitally important in understanding events of the end. Read Psalm 10 as it speaks of the Antichrist. Verse 15 shows a division of his name as we will see also in Thessalonians. "Wicked" refers to the "son of perdition" and "evil man" to the "man of sin". He is the **evil man of sin** in the first half who deceives through a facade of peace. After his death, he is known as the **wicked son of perdition** during the second half that brings death and destruction, the inverse of Jesus who offered **true peace** during His ministry and Everlasting Life after His death.

*"Break thou **the arm** of the **wicked** and the **evil man**: seek out his wickedness till thou find none."*
Psalm 10:15

"Let no man deceive you by any means: for that day shall not come, except there come a falling

*away first, and that **man of sin** be **revealed*** (MoS is revealed *as* the SoP), *the **son of perdition**;" 2 Thess 2:3* (wicked, 2 Thess 2:8)

So, who is the son of perdition? Could it be Judas Iscariot, the one who betrayed our Lord? Jesus said the betrayer would be he whom He gave the SOP (John 13:26). It is interesting how SOP is an acronym for son of perdition. The phrase *"son of perdition"* is written twice in the bible and Jesus directly called Judas the SOP, the first time Satan entered him (Luke 22:3). Perdition means utter loss, destruction. Both "SOP" and "Antichrist" appear exactly four times in the Bible.

> *"While I was with them in the world, I kept them in thy name: those that thou gavest me I have kept, and none of them is **lost, but the son of perdition**; that the scripture might be fulfilled."* John 17:12 (2 Thess 2:3)

> *"...**Judas Iscariot**, which also was the **traitor**."* Luke 6:13

According to Acts 1:25, after Judas hanged himself, he went to what is called his "own place." Could that place have been the bottomless pit, the location in Hell where the fallen angels and hordes of demons come from? Jesus also called Judas a "devil" John 6:70-71.

*"The beast that thou sawest **was**, and **is not**; and **shall ascend out of the bottomless pit**, and **go into perdition**: and they that dwell on the earth shall wonder..."* Rev 17:8

*"And the beast **that was**, and **is not**, even he is the eighth, and is of the seven, and **goeth into perdition**.*" Revelation 17:11

Speaking of Antichrists, John said, *"...but they went out, that they might be **made manifest**..."* 1 John 2:18-19. Judas also went immediately out, *"He then having received the **sop went immediately out**: and it was **night** (into perdition)."* John 13:30. Jesus said the flock would scatter just before His sacrifice, but Judas left the flock completely.

*Then saith Jesus unto them, All ye shall be offended because of me this night: for it is written, I will smite the shepherd, and the **sheep of the flock** shall be **scattered abroad**. Matthew 26:31*

Woe to the idol shepherd that **leaveth the flock!** Zec 11:17

THE SONG OF MOSES: A PROPHETIC WARNING

Before the death of Moses, God spoke with him commanding to write a song and teach it the children of Israel. This song, not only meant for their immediate generation, will be sung again during the Tribulation offering valuable insights into that future period. The Song of Moses stands as a prophetic unveiling of the evil the children of Israel will commit at the "time of the end". Throughout their history, the Israelites repeatedly broke their covenant with God. The pattern of disobedience is prophesied to continue into the Tribulation. The song serves as both a warning and a witness, emphasizing the seriousness of turning away from God and the consequences that follow.

*"And the LORD said unto Moses, Behold, thou shalt sleep with thy fathers; and this people will **rise up, and go a whoring after the gods** of the strangers of the land, whither they go to be among them, and will **forsake me, and break my***

covenant which I have made with them." Deut 31:16.

*"Now therefore **write ye this song** for you, and **teach it the children of Israel:** put it in their mouths, that this song may be **a witness for me against the children of Israel.** For when I shall have **brought them into the land** which I sware unto their fathers, that floweth with milk and honey; and they shall have eaten and filled them-selves, and waxen fat; then will they **turn unto other gods, and serve them,** and **provoke me, and break my covenant.**" Deut 31:19-20*

*"Moses therefore **wrote this song the same day,** and **taught** it the children of Israel" Deut 31:22*

The song was kept with the rest of the law in the Ark of Covenant. Moses spoke to the people all the words of the song.

*"Gather unto me all the elders of your tribes, and your officers, that I may **speak these words** in their ears, and call heaven and earth to **record against them.** For I know that after my death ye will <u>**utterly corrupt**</u> yourselves, and **turn aside** from the way which I have commanded you; and evil will befall you in the <u>latter days</u>; because ye will **do evil in the sight of the LORD,** to **provoke***

him to anger through the <u>work of your hands</u>. (they will make images of the beast) And Moses spake in the ears of all the congregation of Israel the words of this song, until they were ended." Deut 31:28-30

*"They shall be ashamed, and also confounded, all of them: they shall **go to confusion together** that are **makers of idols**."* Is 45:16

The Song of Moses begins in Deuteronomy chapter 32, but only the portion pertaining to the latter days is posted here for discussion.

*"For they are a **nation void of counsel**, neither is there **any understanding in them**. O that they were wise, that they understood this, that they would **consider their <u>latter</u> <u>end</u>!** How should one chase a thousand, and two put ten thousand **to flight**, except their **Rock** had **sold them**,* (turned them over to the AC) *and the LORD had **shut them up?*** (as sheep for the slaughter) *For their rock (Satan) is not as our **Rock**, (Jesus) even our enemies themselves being judges. **For their vine is of the vine of Sodom**,* (degenerate plant of a strange vine, Jer 2:21) *and of the **fields of Gomorrah**: their grapes are **grapes of gall**,* (beareth gall and wormwood, Deut 29:18) *their clusters are **bitter**:* (bitterness

in the latter end, 2 Sam 2:26) *Their wine is the poison of dragons, and the cruel **venom of asps.** (Rom 3:13)* Is not this laid up in store with me, and sealed up among my treasures?

*To me **belongeth vengeance,** and recompence; **their foot shall slide in due time:** for the **day of their calamity is at hand,** and the **things that shall come upon them make haste.** For the **LORD** shall **judge his people,** and **repent himself** for his servants, **when he seeth** that their **power is gone,*** (remnant flees to the wilderness) *and there is **none shut up, or left.*** (none left in the cities and outskirts)

*And he shall say, Where are their **gods,*** (Satan, AC) ***their rock** (AC) in whom **they trusted,** Which did eat the fat of their sacrifices, and drank the wine of their drink offerings? let them rise up and help you, and be your protection. See now that I, even I, am he, and there is no god with me: **I kill, and I make alive;*** (possibly reference to the death of AC, Rev 13:3) ***I wound, and I heal:** neither is there any that can deliver out of my hand.*

*For I lift up my hand to heaven, and say, I live for ever. If I **whet my glittering sword,** and mine hand take hold on **judgment;** I will render **vengeance*** *to mine enemies,* (judgements of Revelation) *and will **reward them that hate me.*** (great winepress) *I will make mine arrows drunk with blood, and my **sword shall devour flesh;** (Rev 19:15) and that with the blood of the slain and of the captives, from the beginning of revenges upon the enemy.*

*Rejoice, **O ye nations, with his <u>people</u>:** (Jews in Israel and around the world during the Tribulation) for he will **avenge the blood of his servants,** (144,000, Rev 6:10, 7:3) and will render vengeance to his adversaries, and will be merciful unto his land, and to his people." Deut 32:28-43*

The Jewish people trusted in many gods over the course of their history, but in the end, they will trust in the vilest god of all, "their rock in whom they trusted". Understanding the reasons behind the Jewish rulers' trust in the Antichrist during the signing of the seven-year covenant is crucial. The leaders of Israel will place their confidence in the promises and assurances of a broken covenant that will be **confirmed** again (Dan 9:27) or reinstated by the AC, believing that this agreement will secure peace and safety for their nation (1 Thess 5:3). However, it is essential to recognize that, even as they enter this covenant, there will be an awareness among the rulers that divine judgments are imminent. The act of signing the covenant will not just be a political maneuver but will also carry with it a sense of foreboding, as the Jewish leaders somehow perceive that they are entering a time when God's judgments are about to unfold. This awareness highlights the magnitude of their decision setting the stage for the events that follow. Following are verses to address these statements.

*"But the word of the LORD was unto them precept upon precept, precept upon precept; line upon line, line upon line; here a little, and there a little; that they might go, and **fall backward**,* (Gen 49:17, fall backward) *and be **broken**, and **snared**, and **taken**.* (Deut 32:35, their foot shall slide in due time)

*Wherefore hear the word of the LORD, **ye scornful men, that rule this people** which is in **Jerusalem**. Because ye have said, We have made a **covenant with death, and with hell*** (Rev 6:8, death and hell) *are we **at agreement**; when the **overflowing scourge*** (judgements) *shall pass through, it **shall not come unto us**: for we have made **lies our refuge**, and under **falsehood** have we **hid ourselves**:*

*Therefore thus saith the Lord GOD, Behold, I lay in Zion for a foundation a stone, a tried stone, a precious corner stone, a sure foundation: **he that believeth** shall <u>**not**</u> **make haste**.* (will make haste, Deut 32:35) *Judgment also will I lay to the* *line, and righteousness to the plummet: and **the hail shall sweep away the refuge of lies**, and the waters shall overflow the hiding place.*

*And your **covenant with death shall be disannulled**, and your **agreement with hell shall not stand;** when the overflowing scourge shall pass through, then **ye shall be trodden down by it.*** (Dan 8:13, trodden) *From the time that it goeth forth it shall take you:* (7 years) *for morning by morning shall it pass over, by day and by night: and it shall be a vexation only to understand the report." Is 28:13-19*

After Moses recited the song, he gave a blessing to each of the twelve tribes and said of Dan, *"And of Dan he said, **Dan is a lion's whelp**: he shall **leap from Bashan."*** Deut 33:22. Meaning, the AC will come from Syria as the **King of the North** (mentioned 7 times) as outlined in Daniel chapter eleven. The only other tribe that was called a lion's whelp was the tribe of Judah. *"Judah is a **lion's whelp:** from the prey, my son, thou art gone up: he stooped down, he couched as a lion, and as an old lion; who shall rouse him up?" Genesis 49:9.* Meaning, from the tribe of Judah shall come Jesus, the Son of God and from Dan shall come Judas, the son of perdition, the son of Satan.

*"**Dan shall judge his people,** as one of the tribes*

of Israel." Genesis 49:16

*"**Dan shall be a serpent** by the way, an adder in the path, that **biteth the horse heels**, (Gen 3:15, heel) so that his rider shall **fall backward**." Genesis 49:17 (Is 28:13, fall backward)*

*"And the **children of Dan** set up the **graven image:" Judges 18:30 (provoke him to anger through the work of your hands, Deut 31:29)*

Of the 144,000 virgins, the tribe of Dan is omitted. The Antichrist will be of Jewish descent which serves as a primary reason the Jewish leaders will initially place their trust in him. Their confidence in the Antichrist at the outset is rooted in his shared heritage, making him appear as a familiar and acceptable figure to represent their interests. This background will play a significant role in persuading the leaders of Israel that entering a covenant with him will secure their peace and safety during tumultuous times. In the end, the people will realize their grave mistake and once again sing the Song of Moses.

*And I saw another sign in heaven, great and marvellous, seven angels having the seven **last** plagues; for in them is filled up the **wrath of God**. And I saw as it were a sea of glass mingled with fire: and them that had gotten the **victory over the beast**, and over **his image**, and over **his mark**, and* *over the **number of his name**, stand on the sea of glass, having the harps of God. And **they sing the song of Moses** the servant of God, and the song of the Lamb, saying, Great and marvellous are thy works, Lord God Almighty; just and true are thy ways, thou King of saints. Rev 15:1-3*

In that day *shall the branch of the LORD be beautiful and glorious, and the fruit of the earth* **shall be excellent** *and comely* **for them that are escaped of Israel.** *Is 4:2*

There is a specific period referred to as the *"hour of temptation"*, which is destined to come upon the entire world. This time of testing is of such unparalleled evil and blasphemy that it is described as a point when *"there remaineth no more sacrifice for sins"* marking a period of ultimate spiritual peril and *apostasy*.

Scripture provides a promise to those who have remained faithful will not have to endure this temptation: *"Because thou hast **kept the word of my patience**, I also will keep thee from the **hour of temptation**, which shall come upon <u>all the world</u>, to **try them** that dwell upon the earth" (Revelation 3:10).* This verse emphasizes that the hour of temptation is not localized, but universal, affecting all who dwell on the earth, both Jews and Gentiles alike. During this time, the Jewish people (and Gentiles) will fully corrupt themselves (Deut 31:29, *utterly corrupt*).

Undoubtedly, during the Tribulation, the Jewish

people will read the New Testament desperately looking for answers. It is no coincidence the official title of one NT book is entitled **"To the Hebrews"**. Nor is it a coincidence the book has thirteen chapters total; the biblical number referring to sin, death, and judgement. The book of Hebrews argues for the superiority of Jesus Christ and the New Testament He established compared to the Old Testament. The book was written to the Jewish Christians of that day but will provide vital understanding for the Jewish people once again in the end. Hebrews chapter 10 is the pivotal chapter in the Book of Hebrews. It concludes the book's main doctrinal argument about the superiority of Christ's sacrifice and priesthood pointing out the insufficiency of Old Covenant sacrifices and the perfection of Christ's sacrifice. This chapter also contains an extreme warning against **willful sin**. Read the entire chapter for context.

Paul is considered the author by most for the book of Hebrews. Just prior to the warning, Paul brings to light the Holy Ghost as a witness for the Church and the new covenant He will make for the writing of the law into the hearts of the Jewish people. This prophecy was also mentioned in Jeremiah 31:31-34.

> For **by one offering** he hath **perfected for ever** them that are sanctified. Whereof the **Holy Ghost also is a <u>witness</u>** to us: for after that he had said

*before, This is the **covenant** that I will **make with them after those days**, saith the Lord, I will **put my laws into their hearts**, and in their minds will I **write** them; And their sins and iniquities will I remember no more. Now **where remission** of these is, there is **no more offering for sin**.* Heb 10:14-18

Paul goes on to say, *"Having therefore, brethren, boldness to enter into the holiest **by the blood of Jesus**, ... " "Let us **hold fast the profession of our faith** without wavering; (for he is faithful that promised;) And let us consider one another to provoke unto love and to good works: **Not forsaking the assembling** of ourselves together, as the manner of some is; but exhorting one another: and so much the more, **as ye see the day approaching**."* Heb 10:19, 23-25. In this passage, Paul is speaking to believers to stand firm in their faith and to assemble with like believers even more *"as ye see the day approaching"*. That day approaching **is** the Day of Christ.

Paul immediately changes his audience in the very next verse, for now he is speaking to those left behind **after** the Day of Christ.

*For if we __sin wilfully__ after that we have __received__ the __knowledge of the truth, there remaineth no more sacrifice for sins,__ But a **certain fearful looking for of judgment** and fiery indignation, which* *shall **devour the adversaries.** He that despised Moses' law **died without mercy under two or three witnesses:** Of how much **sorer punishment,** suppose ye, shall he be thought worthy, who hath **trodden under foot the Son of God,** and hath **counted the blood of the covenant,** wherewith he was sanctified, **an unholy thing,** and hath done despite unto the <u>Spirit of grace</u>? (1 John 5:6, Spirit is witness) For we know him that hath said, **Vengeance** belongeth unto me, **I will recompense,** saith the Lord. And again, **The Lord shall judge his people.** It is a fearful thing to **fall into the hands** of the **living God.** Heb 10:26-31*

There is only one sin that cannot be forgiven, "*Wherefore I say unto you, All manner of sin and blasphemy shall be forgiven unto men: **but the blasphemy against the Holy Ghost shall <u>not</u> be forgiven** unto men.*" Matthew 12:31. The name of the beast (AC) that rises from the sea is blasphemy. "*And I stood upon the sand of the sea, and saw **a beast rise up out of the sea,** having seven heads and ten horns, and upon his horns ten crowns, and upon his heads the <u>**name**</u> of <u>**blasphemy**</u>*" Revelation 13:1.

In Hebrews 10:15, Paul said the Spirit of grace is a witness to us and in verse 28 he said, "*He that despised Moses' law **died without mercy** under two or three **witnesses***". In verse 29 Paul is saying those that **blaspheme against the**

Holy Ghost will receive a **sorer punishment** for what they have done even as the **Spirit of Grace** is still active.

The 144,000 will have a special mission to reach every living soul and preach the **testimony of Jesus Christ** and each virgin will have another with him to complete a minimum of two witnesses. One other witness is the **Holy Ghost**, the **Spirit of grace**, for the 144,000 will witness by the **power** of the **Holy Ghost** so that all the world is <u>**without excuse**</u>. Those that **sin willfully** and **blaspheme** the Holy Ghost and *"received not the love of the truth"*, will *fall away* and fail the *hour of temptation* when they see the ***strong delusion,*** *(and his **deadly wound was healed**: and <u>all</u> <u>the</u> <u>world</u> <u>wondered</u> <u>after</u> the <u>beast</u>" Revelation 13:3)* <u>fallen away</u> from the saving blood of Jesus after which, <u>there remaineth no more sacrifice for sins.</u>

THE DAY OF CHRIST IS AT HAND

Prior to reviewing 2 Thessalonians chapter 2, a main passage that provides an overlay for the time of the end, the term "falling away" must first be defined. Before we look at that specific term used once in 2 Thessalonians, we can look at the companion terms to define the meaning. In brief, the falling away refers to those no longer redeemable by the blood of Christ.

The term *"fell away"* is used three times in the Old Testament; 2 Kings 25:11, Jeremiah 39:9, and Jeremiah 52:15. Each instance refers to the time when King Nebuchadnezzar conquered the southern kingdom of Israel and brought an end to the nation due to their idolatry, covenant unfaithfulness, and misplaced reliance on foreign powers, Egypt in particular, instead of reliance on God. In other words, God gave them over to another. In the end, God will give the unbelieving world over to the Antichrist. The entry for 2 Kings posted below.

> *And in the fifth month, on the seventh day of the month, which is the nineteenth year of king **Nebuchadnezzar king of Babylon**, came Nebuzar-adan, captain of the guard, a servant of the king of Babylon, unto Jerusalem: And he burnt the house of the LORD, and the king's house, and all the houses of Jerusalem, and every great man's house burnt he with fire. And all the army of the Chaldees, that were with the captain of the guard, brake down the walls of Jerusalem round about. Now the rest of the people that were left in the city, and the fugitives that <u>**fell away to the king of Babylon**</u>, with the remnant of the multitude, did Nebuzar-adan the captain of the guard carry away. 2 Kings 25:8-11*

The next term, *"fall away"* used twice in the New Testament, is perhaps more telling. The first instance is from Luke 8 concerning the parable of the seed. The passage speaks for itself but note in the passage the term "time of temptation" is used; the ultimate fulfillment will become *"the hour of temptation" (Rev 3:10)*. The Kingdom of God has already been defined.

> *And when much people were gathered together, and were come to him out of every city, he spake by a **parable**: A **sower went out to sow his seed**: and as he sowed, some fell by the way side; and*

it was <u>*trodden down*</u>, *and the* **fowls of the air** *(unclean spirits) devoured it. And some fell upon a rock; and as soon as it was sprung up,* **it with-ered away, because it** <u>**lacked**</u> **moisture** *(perhaps the Holy Spirit). And some fell among thorns; and the thorns sprang up with it, and choked it. And other fell on good ground, and sprang up, and bare fruit an hundredfold. And when he had said these things, he cried, He that hath ears to hear, let him hear.And his disciples asked him, saying, What might this parable be? And he said, Unto you* **it is given** *to know the* **mysteries of the kingdom of God**: *but to* **others in parables;** *that seeing they* **might not see,** *and hearing they* **might not understand.** *Now the parable is this: The* **seed is the word of God.** *Those by the way side are* **they that hear; then cometh the devil, and taketh away the word** *out of their hearts,* **lest they should believe** *and be saved. They on the rock are they, which, when they hear, receive the word with joy; and* **these have no root, which for a while believe, and in time of temptation** <u>**fall away**</u>. *And that which fell among thorns are they, which, when they have heard, go forth, and are choked with cares and riches and pleasures of this life, and bring no fruit to perfection. But that* **on the good ground are they, which in an honest and** *good* heart, *having <u>heard</u> <u>the</u> <u>word</u>, keep it, and bring forth fruit with patience. Luke 8:9-15*

The second instance of "fall away" is a hotly contested passage even though Paul makes it very clear the meaning. In Hebrews 6 we see the blasphemy of the Holy Ghost from which one cannot be **renewed;** they are left unredeemable.

*For it is <u>**impossible**</u> for those who were **once** enlightened, and have tasted of the heavenly gift, and were **made partakers** of the **Holy Ghost**, And have tasted the good word of God, and the powers of the world to come, If they <u>shall</u> <u>fall</u> <u>away</u>, to renew them again unto repentance; seeing they crucify to themselves the Son of God afresh, and put him to an open shame. Hebrews 6:4-6*

2 Thessalonians chapter 2:1-17 is perhaps one of the most quoted passages in the bible; specifically, for those looking for the rapture. This chapter provides incredible insight into the Time of the End. Hopefully the reader can put together everything that has been discussed up to this point to gain a more informed understanding of this passage.

*1 "Now we **beseech** (implore) you, brethren, by the coming of our Lord Jesus <u>Christ</u>, and by our <u>gathering</u> together unto him,*

2 That ye be not soon shaken in mind, or be troubled, (regarding the Rapture) *neither by spirit, nor by word, nor by letter as from us, as that the* **<u>Day of Christ</u>** *is at hand* (about to happen).

*3 Let no man **deceive you*** (timing of Rapture) *by any means: for **that day*** (Rapture) ***shall not come,*** **<u>except</u>** (excluded, not part of, separate) *there come a falling away <u>first</u>* (rejection of 144,000's message), **<u>and</u>** *that **man of sin*** (called man of sin 1st half and dies) *be **revealed,** the **son of perdition;*** (revealed as the SoP in 2nd half, Dan 9:27, 12:11) (see chapter 5 for naming of AC)

*4 Who opposeth and exalteth himself above all that is called God, or that is worshipped; so that he as God **sitteth*** (on the mercy seat) ***in the temple of God, shewing himself** that he is God."* (son of perdition, 2nd half of Tribulation) **2 Thess 2:1-4**

"At hand", refers to something that is about to take place in the near future. The Thessalonians were afraid they would miss the day, but Paul tells them otherwise. We must rightly divide the Word of God. The key word in the passage above is ***"except"***. Its use in this context means to exclude, not part of, left out. Following are some examples.

*"I tell you, Nay: but, **except ye repent,** ye shall all likewise **perish.**" Luke 13:5* – one cannot perish if they

repent. Repentance is not related to, not part of perishing, it is excluded. Another example: *"Examine yourselves, **whether ye be in the faith**; prove your own selves. Know ye not your own selves, how that **Jesus Christ is in you**, **except** ye **be reprobates**? But I trust that ye shall know that **we are not reprobates**"* 2 Cor 13:5-6. It is one or the other; Christ cannot be in you if you are a reprobate. They are **not** connected. One more for good measure: *"Behold, I will cast her into a bed, and them that commit adultery with her **into great tribulation, except** they **repent** of their deeds."* Revelation 2:22.

Another way to look at it; the preposition "except" separates light from darkness as they have no agreement with each other. **Repentance** (light) separates from **perishing** (darkness). It is also a separation of the two time periods, The Day of Christ (Rapture) and the Tribulation when first, the falling away begins as the 144,000 preach and are rejected, and then the Man of Sin is revealed. Yes, the Church has regressed as the scriptures say but is not utterly corrupt. If it is the Church that **falls away, utterly corrupted, unredeemable**, then the gates of hell have prevailed. *"And I say also unto thee, That thou art Peter, and upon this rock **I will build my church; and the gates of hell shall <u>not</u> prevail** against it."* Matt 16:18. The Word of God defines itself.

The correct order: if the Thessalonians were a witness to see the falling away **and** the man of sin revealed, **then** that day had **already come** and they **missed it**; period. The "falling away" is the blaspheming of the Holy Ghost by the unbelieving Jews and Heathen; no longer redeemable.

The **world** had fallen away once previously. During the days of Noah, the Earth and the entire population of earth had corrupted themselves by allowing the altering of their DNA with the wicked angels, **falling away** from the saving faith in God. Only Noah and his immediate family remained pure. *"These are the generations of Noah: Noah was a just man and perfect in his generations, and Noah walked with God. And Noah begat three sons, Shem, Ham, and Japheth. The <u>earth also</u> was <u>corrupt</u> before God, and the earth was filled with violence. And God looked upon the earth, and, behold, it was <u>corrupt</u>; for <u>all flesh</u> had <u>corrupted</u> his way upon the earth. And God said unto Noah, The end of all flesh is come before me; for the earth is filled with violence through them; and, behold, I will destroy them with the earth."* Genesis 6:9-13

Moses predicted this would happen again in the latter days when he delivered the Song of Moses – *"For I know that after my death ye will <u>utterly corrupt</u> yourselves..."* Deuteronomy 31:29 and we see a similar passage play out in Isaiah during the Tribulation:

*"The land shall be **utterly emptied**, and **utterly spoiled**: for the LORD hath spoken this word. The earth mourneth and **fadeth away**, the world languisheth and fadeth away, the **haughty people of the earth do languish**. The earth also is **defiled** under the inhabitants thereof; because they have **transgressed the laws**, **changed the ordinance**, <u>**broken the everlasting covenant**</u>. Therefore hath the **curse devoured the earth**, and they that dwell therein are desolate: therefore the inhabitants of the earth are burned, and **few men left**. The **new wine mourneth*** (blood of Christ), *the **vine languisheth*** (Jesus, *John 15:5), all the merry-hearted do sigh." Isaiah 24:3-7*

Paul tells the Thessalonians to remember the things he told them when he was there the first time. He does not mention what those things were but perhaps some may be disclosed as we study and read the scriptures to *"...search out a matter" Proverbs 25:2.*

5 "Remember ye not, that, when I was yet with you, I told you these things?

*6 And now ye know **what withholdeth** (God) that he (Man of Sin) **might be revealed** (mid-point) in his time.*

*7 For the **mystery of iniquity** (Satan) **doth already work:** (from the time Eve was enticed in the garden producing rebellion against God) only he (God) who **now letteth will let,** (allow iniquity to continue) **until** he (man of sin, 1st half) be **taken out of the way** (possibly killed by 2 Witnesses) (The wicked are "taken out of the way" Job 24:24)*

*8 And **then** (after man of sin is taken out) shall that **Wicked** (SoP) ("wicked" Job 24:6,24) **be revealed,** whom **the Lord shall consume** with the spirit of his mouth, and **shall destroy** with the brightness of his coming: (Is 11:4, slay the wicked)*

*9 **Even him** (SoP), whose coming is after the working of Satan with **all** power and signs and **lying** wonders," (Rev 13:2) **2 Thess 2:5-9.***

Paul is saying the devil, the "mystery of iniquity", has always been at work, but now God will **letteth** him **unrestrained** as water pouring out via the Antichrist, violently try and gain superiority (via strife) and allow the Antichrist to do so **until** God takes him out. *"The beginning of strife is as when one **letteth** out water: therefore leave off **contention,** before it be meddled with. He that **justifieth the wicked,** and he that **condemneth the just,** even they **both*** *are abomination to the LORD"* Proverbs 17:14-15. It is God that letteth and God that fights for His people. *"For the LORD your God is he that goeth with you, to fight for you against your enemies, to save you"* Deuteronomy 20:4.

10 And with all deceivableness of unrighteousness in them that perish; because they <u>received not</u> (falling away) *the love of the <u>truth</u>,* (message of the 144,000) *that they might be saved.* (this verse may also apply to those that heard and rejected the gospel during Church age as Rom 1:16-18 suggest)

11 And for this cause God shall send them strong delusion: (man of sin is killed and is revived, "the world wondered after the beast" *Rev 13:3), that they should believe a lie: ("and he (*False Prophet*) exerciseth all the power of the first beast before him, and causeth the earth and them which dwell therein to worship the first beast, whose deadly wound was healed. Rev 13:12)*

12 That they all might be damned who <u>believed not</u> (falling away) *the truth, but had pleasure in unrighteousness. (For the wrath of God is revealed from heaven against all ungodliness and* *unrighteousness of men, who **hold the <u>truth</u> in unrighteousness**; Rom 1:18)*

*13 But we are bound to give thanks alway to God for you, **brethren beloved of the Lord,** because God hath from the beginning chosen you to salvation through sanctification of the Spirit and <u>**belief of the truth**</u>:* (Paul has circled back to the Church at this point encouraging them once more)

*14 Whereunto he called you by **our gospel** (gospel of Christ), to the **obtaining of the glory** of our Lord Jesus **Christ.***

*15 Therefore, brethren, **stand fast,** and **hold the traditions** which ye have been taught, whether by word, or our epistle. 16 Now our Lord Jesus Christ himself, and God, even our Father, which hath loved us, and hath given us **everlasting consolation** and **good hope** through grace, 17 **Comfort your hearts,** and stablish you in every good word and work. 2 **Thess 2:1-17***

As mentioned previously in chapter 3, *"the Day of Christ is at hand"* **is not** a mistranslation of the Day of the Lord as many have said. In the passage below, Paul <u>is</u> speaking about the **Day of the Lord.** Notice the darkness and negative tone it presents. On the flip side, there is nothing negative or dark concerning "the coming of our Lord

Jesus Christ and by our gathering together unto him", but rather, it is **the escape** from it.

> *"But of the times and the seasons, brethren, ye have no need that I write unto you. For yourselves know perfectly that the* **day of the Lord** *so* **cometh as a <u>thief</u> in the night.** *For when they shall say, Peace and safety; then* **sudden destruction cometh upon them,** *as travail upon a woman with child; and they* **shall <u>not</u> escape."** *1 Thess 5:1-3*

Dear reader – if you have yet to put your trust in the **blood of Jesus Christ** and escape the coming destruction, it is not too late. For the **Day of Christ is at hand** now more than ever. If you choose to delay and miss that day, you will face the coming Tribulation or the Great White Throne Judgement (last day below) and be **cast** into the **Lake of Fire.**

> *"***Jesus** *cried and* **said,** *He that believeth on me, believeth not on me, but on him that sent me. And he that seeth me seeth him that sent me. I* **am come a light into the world, that whosoever believeth on me should not abide in <u>darkness</u>.** *And if any man hear my words, and believe not, I judge him not: for I came not to judge the world, but to* **save the world.** *He that* **rejecteth me, and receiveth not my words, hath one that judgeth***

*him: the word that I have spoken, **the same shall judge him in the <u>last day</u>**. For I have not spoken of myself; but the Father which sent me, he gave me a commandment, what I should say, and what I should speak. And I know that **his commandment is life everlasting:** whatsoever I speak therefore, even as the Father said unto me, so I speak."*
John 12:44-50

*"For unto us a child is born, unto us a son is given: and the **government shall be upon his shoulder:** and his name shall be called Wonderful, Counsellor, The mighty God, The everlasting Father, The Prince of Peace. Of the <u>increase</u> of **his government** and peace there **shall be <u>no end</u>, upon the throne of David**, and upon **his kingdom,** to order it, and to establish it with judgment and with justice from henceforth even **for ever.** The zeal of the LORD of hosts will perform this." Isaiah 9:6-7*

Amen.

The Time of The End
Day of Christ
Rapture of the Church 2 Thess 2:1-2
Tribulation Commences
Dan 9:27 Man of Sin
Sealing of the 144,000
Rev 7:1-5
5th Seal
144,000 martyred Rev 6:9 Man of Sin killed Rev 13:3,12,14 War in Heaven, Satan cast into the earth. Rev 12:7-9
Mid-point revealing of the Man of Sin
Beast rises from sea/bottomless pit as the Son of Perdition after the Man of Sin is revived from death and revealed Rev 13:1-3 Rev 17:8 AC kills 2 Witnesses Rev 11:7
Directly after Revealing
The Hour of Temptation to worship the Beast after Man of Sin is revived from death, strong delusion Rev 3:10 Rev 13:4 Remaineth no more sacrifice for sins Heb 10:26
Day of the Lord
Isaiah 13:6 Joel 1:15 2 Peter 3:10
Preparation for KoH
Sheep & Goat Judgement Matt 25:31-46 Marriage & Supper of the Lamb Building of Millennial Temple Ez 40-48
Kingdom of Heaven
Millennial Reign of Christ Rev 20:4 Great White Throne Judgement at end Rev 20:11-15
Eternity
The Father's Kingdom New Heaven & New Earth Rev 21:1
Year 1
The Falling Away - Heathen
Blasphemy of the Holy Ghost
Mid-point
Year 7
1,000 Years

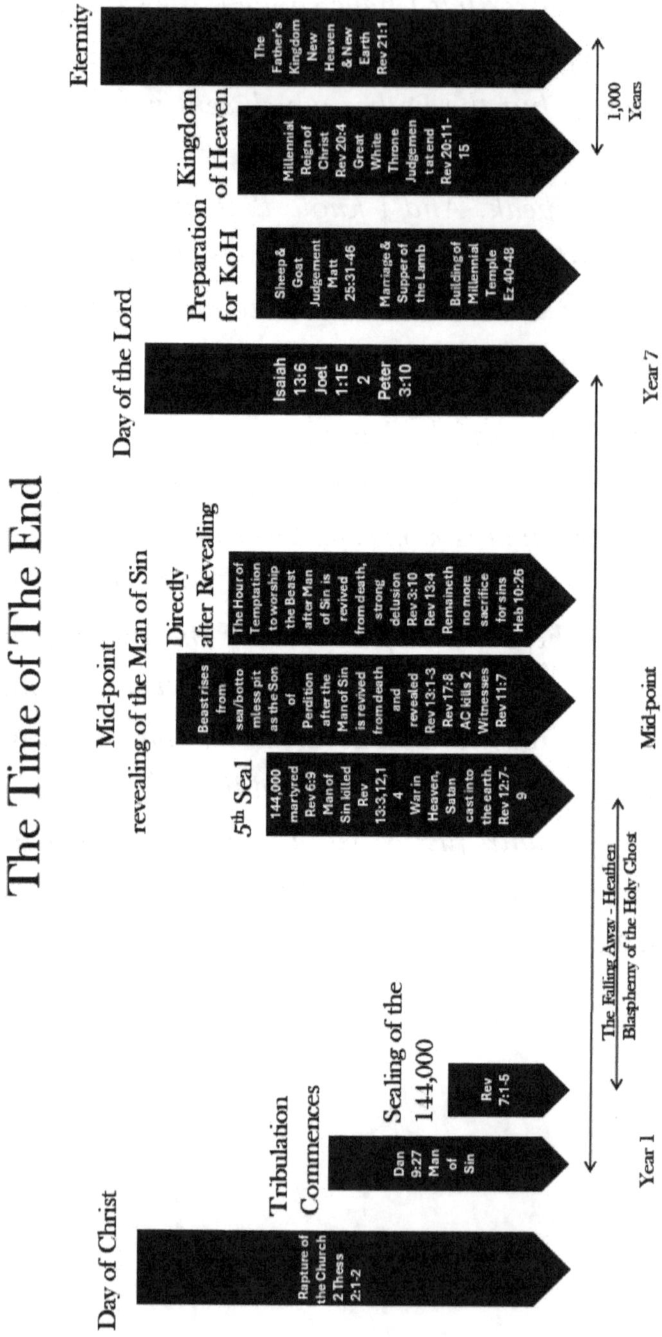

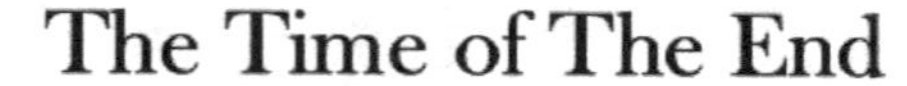

ALSO NEW FROM ALAN T. HARRIS

How it all began and the origin of sin. Travel back to the very beginning of creation to learn the history of the great dragon and how it leads up to the "Time of the End".